The Economics of the Yasuní Initiative

The Economics of the Yasuní Initiative

Climate Change as if Thermodynamics Mattered

JOSEPH HENRY VOGEL

FOREWORD BY
GRACIELA CHICHILNISKY

ANTHEM PRESS
LONDON · NEW YORK · DELHI

Anthem Press
An imprint of Wimbledon Publishing Company
www.anthempress.com

This edition first published in UK and USA 2009
by ANTHEM PRESS
75-76 Blackfriars Road, London SE1 8HA, UK
or PO Box 9779, London SW19 7ZG, UK
and
244 Madison Ave. #116, New York, NY 10016, USA

Prologue © 2009 by José Manuel Hermida
Foreword © 2009 by Graciela Chichilnisky
Introduction, Acknowledgements, Chapters 1–5,
Conclusions, Notes © 2009 by Joseph Henry Vogel
Filmography © 2009 by Janny Robles

The moral right of the authors has been asserted.

British Library Cataloguing in Publication Data
A catalogue record for this book is available from the British Library.

Library of Congress Cataloging in Publication Data
A catalog record for this book has been requested.

ISBN-13: 978 1 84331 878 1 (Hbk)
ISBN-10: 1 84331 878 4 (Hbk)

ISBN-13: 978 1 84331 874 3 (Pbk)
ISBN-10: 1 84331 874 1 (Pbk)

ISBN-13: 978 1 84331 863 7 (eBook)
ISBN-10: 1 84331 863 6 (eBook)

1 3 5 7 9 10 8 6 4 2

To the people of the 22nd century

"[T]his most excellent canopy, the air, look you, this brave o'erhanging firmament, this majestical roof fretted with golden fire – why, it appeareth nothing to me but a foul and pestilent congregation of vapors."

—William Shakespeare, *Hamlet*, Act II, scene ii.

CONTENTS

Conclusions:
Reason for Hope and Despair   71

Appendix: Annotated YouTube Filmography   79

PROLOGUE

Ethics and the Economics of Climate Change

Discussion about climate change and the management of CO_2 emissions constitute a global debate for humanity. The causes and effects are the object of intense scientific study by experts who urge immediate and large-scale action. The conversation is largely expressed in terms of economics and development with little contemplation of the ethics of the present predicament.

Until now the proposed solutions have usually relied on the application of market instruments to the scarce capacity of the atmosphere – a global public good – to cycle greenhouse gases. Less discussed are the asymmetries among countries regarding excessive emissions and the consequences suffered. Almost absent is the perspective of political economy.

Into this scenario arrives *The Economics of the Yasuní Initiative*. It offers a fresh vision, holistic and substantiated, to the dilemmas of climate change. Ethics infuse every page and the tone is defiant. Official discourse is vigorously questioned and thermodynamics is shown to matter, indeed. Physics explains how the atmospheric sink was appropriated in the North and economics, how payment for foregoing petroleum extraction in the South can lead to both efficiency and equity.

The Yasuní-ITT Initiative emerges from Ecuador where the concept of *buen vivir* (good living) is forging a new relationship for government, society, nature and the market. The proposal finds itself in a milieu unimaginable just a few years ago: the conferring of rights to nature under the Ecuadorian Constitution of November 2008 – an earnest attempt to restore our environment.

The Economics of the Yasuní Initiative debuts on the eve of a global summit in Copenhagen, the fifteenth Conference of the Parties to the United Nations Framework Convention on Climate Change. Hopefully, humanity will reach agreement and implement an array of solutions – including the Initiative – which will fulfill the expectations implied in the poignant dedication "to the people of the 22nd century."

José Manuel Hermida
Resident Representative
United Nations Development Programme
Country Office – Ecuador

FOREWORD

Yasuní: The New Economics of Planet Earth

Humans are changing the metabolism of the planet to a degree previously unknown. We are fundamentally altering the gases in the atmosphere, the bodies of water and the complex web of species that constitutes life on Earth. *The Economics of the Yasuní Initiative* appears at a time when the dangers to the world's resources have become clear to the naked eye. Rates of extinction are now 1,000 times higher than the rate inferred from the fossil record. Climate change seems to be accelerating. For humans, this means rising seas, ferocious floods, prolonged droughts and erratic weather patterns. In 2010, we may see over 50 millions climate refugees worldwide. The problem is global in nature. There is nowhere to hide.

Approximately 80% of humanity lives in the developing world, often amidst valuable natural resources. Ecuador is a microcosm of that world and its UNESCO Biosphere Reserve – Yasuní – is exemplary of resources in their original state. However, Yasuní sits atop a huge oil reserve. As is the case in many other carbon-rich developing nations, roughly half of Ecuador lives in poverty. Understandably, the government is tempted to exploit the oil of Yasuní and expand the agricultural frontier simply to feed its population despite the negative global impacts on the environment – just as industrialized countries did at a similar stage of their economic development.

The conflict between basic needs and resource exports is as acute as it is cruel. In the case of Ecuador, the lion's share of export income comes from petroleum sales and the majority of its people enjoy no benefit. It is actually worse for the indigenous communities of the Ecuadorian Amazon. Many live directly from the products of the forest that is systematically destroyed by the extraction of petroleum. Two communities in the Biosphere Reserve live in voluntary isolation much as their ancestors have lived for thousands of years. What will be their fate?

In 1992 I published an article in the *America Economic Review* which explains the case of Ecuador and the damages to the global environment derived from petroleum exports based on a pool of commonly owned natural resources.[1] I showed that the conflict arises from the rapid expansion of international markets where traders are at different stages of development, namely North-South trade. I showed why the inevitable result is market failure at a global scale. A clear pattern of trade had emerged through time and is evident from the data. The exporters of resources were largely pre-industrial nations like Ecuador, whose natural resources are common property while the importers were industrial nations whose resources are private. The divergence leads to a "tragedy of the commons" on an unprecedented global scale, magnified a voracious international market that was in great measure enabled through the Bretton Woods institutions that were created after World War II. In this visible effect of globalization, the traditional controls which once controlled the use of resources locally and offered a solution to the tragedy are now no longer available. Exploitation is often on a first come first serve basis as "open access" conspires with the pressures of poverty. Resources are typically being exported at prices *below* replacement costs.

The over-consumption in the North and over-extraction in the South has created a global environmental disaster, especially in the atmosphere. Discerning the problem, I looked for a solution in an update of conventional economics, and incorporated that thinking as a lead author of the Intergovernmental Panel of Climate Change that would later win the Nobel Peace Prize in 2007. Working with the Lead Negotiator of the Kyoto Protocol, Argentine Ambassador Raul Estrada, and representatives of the OECD and the US administration, I designed the carbon market. Then by request of the French Delegation, I drafted the language of the Kyoto Protocol that launched the carbon market and created the Kyoto Protocol in December 17, 1997.

My method in creating the carbon market is rather novel and was initially controversial. But in reality it reflects an evolution of classical economic thinking. I attempted to rectify the effects of the missing property rights on resources within poor nations by creating global rights on the use of resources by wealthy nations. These would be limits on CO_2 emissions. The framework is grounded in efficiency criteria, once one recognizes the atmosphere as a global public good.[2] After dramatic ups and downs, my solution finally became international law with the ratification by Russia of the Kyoto Protocol in 2005. The results have been both remarkable and measurable. Outstanding among them are the $23 billion in transfers from the developed to developing nations through the Clean Development Mechanism that created clean production projects in poor nations. I am also pleased to see that these projects decreased the equivalent of European Union emissions by 20% and that carbon credits trade at the European Union Trading System now count at $60 billion per year.[3] This means that those who over-emit paid $60 billion to those who under-emit.

Thinking like an economist, I would say that the Kyoto Protocol has fundamentally changed the way we do business – and our economic values – by making CO_2 emissions monetarily costly and clean development finally profitable. The economic change has also been accompanied by a sea change in social psychology. People are demanding that carbon polluters pay. Although still young, Kyoto may be on its last legs. The December 2009 Copenhagen COP XV is a "do or die" meeting for the climate negotiations because the provisions of Kyoto will expire in 2012. I hope that Copenhagen will move the Kyoto Process ahead.

In this context, the Yasuní-ITT Initiative is especially symbolic. How does it fit into the global picture just described? The Initiative is an innovative response from Latin America to the procrastination of the global negotiations. Although it resonates as fair in environmental circles of the North and the South, it resonates especially well in the fossil-fuels rich South. To date, Kyoto has delivered few benefits to the poorest nations in the developing world largely because the Clean Development Mechanism finances projects to reduce existing emissions – which originate mostly from China. Currently, carbon-rich Latin America and Africa emit very little CO_2 (e.g. Africa emits a bare 3% of the world total) and therefore they cannot benefit from reducing emissions. In addition, carbon-rich developing countries do not want to be locked out of the possibility of development through energy-intensive industrialization. What is the alternative?

With the stage now set, one can understand why Rafael Correa, President of Ecuador, proposed in 2007 to the United Nations General Assembly that the international community compensate Ecuador for not extracting the petroleum reserves in the Yasuní Biosphere Reserve. Although the proposal seems simple and has much intuitive appeal, the economics had not yet been worked out. Joseph Henry Vogel was assigned that task and shows in this volume that those economics are not always simple and can often be counterintuitive.

I met Joseph at the University of Puerto Rico in 2009 where he served as a discussant to my keynote presentation on the creation of the carbon market of the Kyoto Protocol. It is my pleasure to reciprocate and discuss his provocative book which I believe will inspire a much needed debate about equity. I reiterate: The Yasuní-ITT Initiative is on target once one recognizes that the global concentration of CO_2 in the atmosphere is a global public good. Ecuador is providing the world a global public good when it refrains from extracting petroleum that causes emissions. I established this general theme in 1992 and on the basis of that work, I would now say that compensation is required should Ecuador refrain from drilling in the Yasuní-ITT fields.[4]

The Yasuní-ITT Initiative can also serve as a global model for carbon-rich but economically poor countries. Some simple statistics can drive home my point: the 80% of humanity who live in the developing world emit only 40% of atmospheric CO_2. The 20% who live in the developed world emit 60%. Simply put, if the developed world emitted CO_2 at the levels of the developing world, we would not now be experiencing climate change. Equity is the crux of this argument and of the arguments in *The Economics of the Yasuní Initiative*.

Jopeph Vogel starts with a critique of neoclassical economics. Perhaps he is right about the importance of thermodynamics for economics, especially in the long run. His argument is that we have neither a closed system nor an equilibrium but an open system in which CO_2 emissions have overwhelmed the atmospheric sink.

Vogel seems right. But do we need to go cosmic here? As evidenced by Venus on the book jacket, Vogel thinks so. His message is directed to an educated reader who may nevertheless be unfamiliar with economic thinking and impatient with all our formalism. However, for the trained economist, the question who should abate carbon emissions or who should compensate whom for using the global commons is well understood within the theory of markets *with public goods that are privately produced*.[5] In neoclassical economics, a recognition of such goods leads to the same general recommendation. In other words, the magnifying effects of international trade where asymmetry exists between parties explains the global tragedy of the commons and the result is climate change. What we need to redress this market failure is to compensate those who produce a positive externality and charge those who produce the negative externality. This is what the carbon market does. This is what, in a different way, the Yasuní-ITT Initiative attempts to do.

The pattern is clear. Markets for public goods are the markets of the future. It is generally believed that the carbon market will soon become the largest commodity market in the world, and trading carbon credits is trading rights to use a global public good. Besides the carbon concentration in the atmosphere, other global public goods include access to genetic resources and the management of watersheds.[6] Markets to limit their use and realize their value are emerging rapidly. Some are already full-fledged. For example, the Chicago Board of Trade has been successfully trading SO_2 for 12 years. Nevertheless *I am not saying that markets are the solution to all global environmental problems*.

Markets are a tool and not a goal. A hazard of interdisciplinary conversation is that we often confuse tools with goals. The goal is to live within a global limit on CO_2 emissions, which in turn can be decomposed into national limits. Markets can be used to send signals to best implement these limits. The global limits come from physics, and perhaps by highlighting thermodynamics, as Vogel does, we will become more sensitized to the physical limits of the Earth's resources. The carbon market is just a useful tool for allocating scarce quantities of allowable CO_2 emissions through prices. And why prices, you may ask? Why impose a global market on an otherwise simple initiative? The answer is obvious. The price mechanism enables compensation for continued avoidance of CO_2 emissions which will thereby safeguard both the habitat of Yasuní and the people who have lived sustainably in that habitat. Despite being a vocal critic of neoclassical economics, even Vogel turns to the price mechanism and ends Chapter Two endorsing a carbon market for the CO_2 avoided through the Initiative. I agree.

Tools are important, and different ways of doing economics can shape our thinking. But the truth will shine through no matter what tool we use. The inseparable link between *climate change* and *inequity* shines through, whether one thinks in traditional economic terms or thinks thermodynamically. By thinking both ways, a synergy emerges. Yasuní is the new economics of planet Earth. As the brilliant image on the book jacket suggests, what is at stake is not just the survival of humankind but of other forms of life as well. Time is running out.

Graciela Chichilnisky
Professor of Economics and Statistics
UNESCO Professor of Mathematics and Economics, 1996–2008
Director, Columbia Consortium for Risk Management
Columbia University, New York City, New York
www.chichilnisky.com

INTRODUCTION

On the 5th of March 2009 I signed a contract with the United Nations Development Programme to be the general evaluator of the Yasuní-ITT Initiative. Yasuní is a UNESCO Biosphere Reserve and a National Park in the Ecuadorian Amazon. Within the park live two indigenous communities who have chosen voluntary isolation, the Tagaere and Taromenane. Below the Park lie the oil fields Isphingo, Tambococha and Tiputini, abbreviated as ITT. Upon learning of just these bare bone facts, I quickly realized that I have been thinking about the economics that justifies the Initiative for almost my entire professional career – long before I knew where Yasuní is and what it will mean for humanity. Drawing on my previous trajectory in the areas of non-equilibrium thermodynamics, biodiversity, and ecocriticism, I offer this short book as the "product" of the consultancy. However, I hope that it will also be an invitation to delve deeper into the arguments referenced in the notes and filmography.

Because climate change is the leading issue of our day, the book is contextualized in the events that transpired from the first of March 2009 to the first of July 2009. These include the G-20 Summit in London, the passage of the "Clean Energy and Security Act of 2009," the Fifth Summit of the Americas in Trinidad and Tobago, the negotiating session in Bonn of the Fifteenth Conference of the Parties to the United Nations Framework Convention on Climate Change, the formal US recognition of greenhouse gases as pollutants, and the passage of the American Clean Energy and Security Act. Coincident with these political events is the frightening news from *Science* that the Amazon is experiencing a drought that could shift the ecosystem from forest to savannah and cause a transition from net absorption to net emission of carbon dioxide.[1]

In surveying a vast technical literature, I have profited immensely from *The Economics of Climate Change: The Stern Review*. If the debate can be conceptualized as a network, *The Stern Review* is its node. Despite stunning success, the author, Sir Nicholas Stern is pluralistic. He ends his *tour-de-force* with this closing sentence "In conclusion we should stress again that the analysis of the Review as a whole was always intended to be one of contribution to a discussion. There have been, will be, and should be many more contributions."[2]

Despite a sincere admiration for Stern, my subtitle *Climate Change as if Thermodynamics Mattered* may seem a parody of his title. It is not. The case that Ecuador be compensated for *not* extracting its petroleum builds on an alternative foundation to resource allocation. My position is that economic theory, cited in the first page of *The Stern Review* (viz., "Climate Change – Our Approach"), has been a "driver" of climate change. Stern writes that climate change "presents a unique challenge for economics: it is the greatest example of market failure we have ever seen."[3] In other words, to solve a problem driven by a theory, we need more of the same theory! I vehemently disagree. Instead of economics-as-usual, the switch to thermodynamics allows us to make a meaningful picture of the sundry studies compiled in *The Stern Review* and begin the public conversation about a problem that has no technical solution. The Yasuní-ITT Initiative is one of the many non-technical solutions that must be vetted.

The five short chapters explore the implications of deploying thermodynamics as the framework for climate change policy. What exactly is the Yasuní-ITT Initiative? In the broadest sense, it is a draft proposal that has been correctly criticized for lacking coherence.[4] More specifically, it is a vision by Rafael Correa, President of Ecuador, that the international community compensate his country for *not* extracting oil from the ITT oil fields of the Yasuní National Park.[5] Why should the international community pay anyone for doing nothing? what should they pay? and how would they pay it? These are some of the questions that I explore in this book. To make the answers cohere requires an alternative approach to climate change, international policy, and sustainable development. To get anyone to listen, requires that I assume the persona of *provocateur*.

I have contextualized my arguments not only in current events but also the long sweep of history. In our age of climate change and mass extinction, a coherent policy framework is a necessary condition for "human prosperity, energy security, and environmental sustainability"[6] but it will never be sufficient. One also needs the recognition of necessity itself. Given the multiple manifestations of human-made crises, the timing for *The Economics of the Yasuní Initiative* could not be better.

Joseph Henry Vogel
Professor of Economics
University of Puerto Rico-Río Piedras
San Juan, Puerto Rico
www.josephhenryvogel.com

ACKNOWLEDGEMENTS

In December 2008, I visited María Fernanda Espinosa, the Permanent Representative of Ecuador to the United Nations at the Consulate-General in New York. The appointment was to discuss my forthcoming anthology *The Museum of Bioprospecting, Intellectual Property, and the Public Domain* for launch at the Tenth Conference of the Parties of the United Nations Convention on Biological Diversity (CBD), scheduled for 2010 in Nagoya, Japan. To my pleasant surprise, Ecuadorian economist Carlos Larrea arrived at the Consulate-General at the same time. The next thing I knew, I was recruited for the Yasuní-ITT Initiative. The thinking of both María Fernanda and Carlos was that my expertise on the CBD would carry over to the United Nations Framework Convention on Climate Change (UNFCCC). The coincidence of Carlos' visit with mine was a chance event, typical of bifurcation points in non-equilibrium thermodynamics. Besides thanking María Fernanda and Carlos for this opportunity, I suppose I should also thank chance itself.

The Office of the United Nations Development Programme (UNDP) in Ecuador formalized my consultancy in March 2009. I thank José Vicente Troya and Anamaría Varea for their commitment to the project. The President of the Yasuní-ITT Commission, Roque Sevilla, allowed me the freedom to write whatever I thought appropriate. Before I agreed, I set only one condition: I must visit the biosphere reserve, deep in the Ecuadorian Amazon. Too often armchair economists suggest policies without ever having visited the place about which they write.

The following week I was off to Yasuní with a group of American university students from the School for International Training (SIT). The logistics were an all-day affair. Besides the plane-hop over the

Andes and some rickety bus rides, there were two boat trips, the last one some three hours long, river bend after bend. We were lodged at the comfortable Tiputini Biological Station run by the University of San Francisco de Quito. I thank Sylvia Seger, director of the SIT program and the ecologist Peggy Stern, also affiliated with SIT. The week was fascinating, rejuvenating, and even detoxifying (e.g. no alcohol permitted at the Tiputini Biological Station). Sylvia tells me that she goes to Yasuní every semester and always observes something new, such is the richness of a "hot spot" of biodiversity. Having now experienced that first-hand, the responsibility weighs heavily. Should the endeavors of the Yasuní-ITT Initiative fail, the magnificence of the reserve will be exchanged for a few days of fueling up cars in the industrialized North. The calculus was explained to me by the SIT co-director Xavier Silva, an ornithologist who somehow maintains good cheer.

One week later, with a mental picture of Yasuní formed, I began writing. Like the serialized stories in the newspapers of yore, *The Economics of the Yasuní Initiative* appeared chapter by chapter. However, the medium of communication was not newsprint but attachments via email. To those on the Commission who did not press the DELETE button or activate a SPAM filter, I express my thanks: Natalia Greene, Carolina Zambrano, Frederico Starnfeld, Andrés Hubenthal, Marcelo Baquero, Olga Cavalucci, and Carina Bracer. Any written text needs feedback, not just in writing but also spoken. So I also wish to thank the attendants who stayed awake to hear my lectures in the following venues and especially thank those who asked pointed questions: Tiputini Biodiversity Station, (Yasuní National Park, Orellana, Ecuador, 15 March 2009); "USA and the Kyoto Protocol post 2012," (University of Puerto Rico-Rio Piedras, 2 April 2009); "Conservation and development trade-offs in Peru," (Lima, Peru, June 24, 2009); the Seminario-Taller Ambiente y Nueva Arquitectura Financiera Regional, (Quito, Ecuador, 6 August 2009); FLACSO Argentina (Buenos Aires, 21 September 2009); and "Cambio Climático y Buen Vivir" (Cochabamba, Bolivia, 10 October 2009).

In the midst of writing the installments, I was invited to collaborate on an article entitled "Leaving the Oil in the Ground: A Political, Economic, and Ecological Initiative in the Ecuadorian Amazon," subsequently published by the Americas Program of The Center for International Policy (Washington, D.C., 13 August 2009). Much of the thinking in my contribution to that article overlaps with this book and I wish to thank my co-authors Esperanza Martínez, Alberto Acosta, and Eduardo Gudynas.

My primary criterion in choosing a publisher for *The Economics of the Yasuní Initiative*, was free internet accessibility from a major press. In vetting the possibilities, I received valuable input from Matt Finer who wrote the first refereed article about the Yasuní-ITT Initiative. James Aronson provided excellent advice from his recent experiences in publishing about tropical biodiversity conservation. The initial contact with Anthem Press was made on the recommendation of Robert Davis of the United Nations University Press.

An eye for detail is the requisite for copyediting and the cleaner the manuscript, the easier the task of the copyeditor. I benefited immensely from the comments of Jerry Hoeg, Paul Baymon, Barbara A. Hocking, Camilo Gomides, Teodora Zamudio, and Maritza Stanchich. They spotted errors, sometimes seemingly small, and made discerning comments. For example, Maritza suggested "pre-literate" rather than "illiterate" in Chapter 4 and the substitution greatly clarifies the meaning. Her hackles were raised by my discussion of family planning in Chapter 5 which induced me to elaborate the argument more fully so that the general readership does not misunderstand.

The choice of the image for the book jacket is mine. Although Earth and Venus, side by side, hazards dismissal of my work as "ultra-Malthusian," I have found no other image that captures so well what is at stake. I would like to thank the NGOs which displayed the poster of the book jacket at the Climate Forum of the fifteenth Conference to the Parties (COPXV) of the UNFCCC. At the COPXV, I enjoyed observer status through my affiliation with Fundación Futuro Latinoamericana of Ecuador and I thank the coordinator, Monica Andrade, and board members Jorge Caillaux and Yolanda Kakabadse.

Special gratitude is expressed toward those organizations which financially helped to make this book available on the web, free of cost. Topping the list is the UNDP-Ecuador. Thanks are also owed to Tej P. S. Sood of Anthem Press for experimenting with an open access book and simultaneous hard and soft cover editions.

Many will not agree with everything in this book (nor should they) but I think all will agree with the urgency to get the planet through the bottleneck of a cowboy economy. This book is my opinion. Through its free accessibility on the web, I hope it will not remain mine alone. Nevertheless, the usual disclaimer applies to both the individuals named here and the institutions that have collaborated in any form.

The final touches to the manuscript were made during the downtime of the First Audience of the International Tribunal of Climate Justice, held in Cochabamba, Bolivia (13–14 October 2009). The venue was the Law School auditorium at the Universidad Mayor de San Simon Bolívar. Hundreds of spectators heard the cases presented before the Tribunal. I served as one of eight jurors. Some cases were heart-breaking and a passion for justice was palpable in the room. On the elevated stage, a table was situated for the jury to face the public. Seated in the center was the presiding jurywoman, the octogenarian Nora Morales de Cortiñas from the Mothers of the Plaza de Mayo (*Linea Fundadora*) of Buenos Aires, Argentina. Her hair was covered with a white scarf embroidered with the date of the disappearance of her son, Carlos Gustavo (15 April 1977). Around her neck, she wore a photo of the then 24 year old Carlos. After we recessed for hours to deliberate the cases, we returned to the auditorium and the audience still numbered in the hundreds. In a clear and forceful voice, each of the jury members read a few paragraphs of the draft ruling.

Nora closed the tribunal. Standing less than five feet tall, she raised her clenched fist and demanded justice for the victims of all international crimes against humanity. Her presence reminded us that climate change is just such a crime. Scanning the auditorium and in the name of the *"desaparecidos,"* she called for their attendance. The audience responded thunderously *¡PRESENTE!*

In the echo, I could also hear the whisper of the still unborn, "presente."

ABBREVIATIONS AND ACRONYMS

ADEA	Age Discrimination in Employment Act of 1967
CBD	Convention on Biological Diversity
CCS	Carbon Capture and Sequestration
CDM	Clean Development Mechanism
CO_2e	Carbon dioxide equivalent
COP	Conference of the Parties
EPA	Environmental Protection Agency
FLACSO	Facultad Latinoamericana de Ciencias Sociales
G-20	Group of Twenty
G-8	Group of Eight
GDP	Gross Domestic Product
HDI	Human Development Index
IPCC	Intergovernmental Panel on Climate Change
ITT	Isphingo, Tambococha and Tiputini
NAMAs	Nationally Appropriate Mitigation Actions
NET	Non-equilibrium thermodynamics
NGOs	Non-governmental Organizations
NIMBY	Not-in-my-back-yard
NIMTO	Not-in-my-term-of-office
OPEC	Organisation of Petroleum Exporting Countries
SIMTO	Solely-in-my-term-of-office
SIT	School for International Training
UNFCCC	United Nations Framework Convention on Climate Change
UN-REDD	United Nations Collaborative Programme on Reducing Emissions from Deforestation and Forest Degradation in Developing Countries
WPA	Works Progress Administration

The Economics of the Yasuní Initiative

Chapter 1
THERMODYNAMICS
The Language Chosen
Defines the Debate

"Sunk costs" is a useful concept. Its definition in economic theory has many expressions in popular speech. The favorites seem to be "don't spend good money after bad" and "let bygones be bygones." In less colloquial language, decisions should be taken on the basis of future benefits related to future costs and not on the basis of past costs. One should not let a poor prior decision color the decision to be taken now. Nevertheless, they do and that is why "sunk costs" is such a useful concept. The seemingly endless American wars in Afghanistan and Iraq are a good example. Politics explains why presidents and prime ministers do not apply the concept of sunk costs. In matters as grave as war, reversal of course is an admission of a monstrous error. So, to avoid paying the political price, the powers-that-be will "kick the can down the road" and ignore the concept of sunk costs. In the case of the simultaneous American wars, the price tag is already estimated in the trillions of dollars.[1]

Economic theory is not much different. Its conceptual framework *now* exhibits sunk costs and nowhere is this more evident than in climate change and the intertwined mass extinction crisis. I italicize the adverb "now" to emphasize that at one time the benefits of the framework were greater than the costs, but that time has long since past. When did it pass? Why did it pass? And what exactly do I mean by economic theory?

Let us examine the last question first. Economic theory is a seductively simple model of resource allocation. Indeed, it is so simple that a thumbnail sketch can do it justice. People are assumed to be rational and will express their self-interest in the marketplace. Through the continuous adjustment of prices and quantities, the allocation of resources steadily moves toward an equilibrium at which point the supply of goods and services equals demand for those goods and services. Introductory textbooks diagram the process as a circular flow where households supply the factors (land, labor, and capital) to the firms which produce the goods and services.[2] Such diagrams come with a caveat found a few pages later, viz., whenever the nature of a good militates against a market transaction (e.g. a lighthouse), either the government should provide it or think of some way to create a market where none previously existed.[3]

With "economic theory" now defined, we return to our initial questions "when did the time for it pass?" and "why did it pass?" A clue lies in entertaining "when did economic theory begin?" and "why did it begin?" In the first chapter to *The Worldly Philosophers*, Robert L. Heilbroner notes "[a]n odd fact: man had struggled with the economic problem since long before the time of the Pharaohs, and in these centuries he had produced philosophers by the score, scientists, political thinkers, historians, artists by the gross, statesmen by the hundred of dozen. Why, then, were there no economists?"[4] The next chapter is entitled "The Economic Revolution" and Heilbroner resolves the enigma: the "agents" of production (viz., tradeable land, employable labor, and fluid capital) were not sufficiently plentiful throughout most of history to make economic theory useful for explaining resource allocation. "Lacking land, labor, and capital, the Middle Ages lacked the market; and lacking the market (despite its colorful local marts and traveling fairs), society ran by custom and tradition."[5] The ecologist would interpret Heilbroner's explanation as one of *scale*. Tradeable land, employable labor, and fluid capital indeed existed before the end of the eighteenth century, but not at the *scale* necessary to account for the allocation of most resources. Just as *scale* is the ultimate answer to "why did economic theory begin?" it is also the answer to "why did the time for it pass?" At some point, the *scale* of pollution, ignored in the circular flow between households and firms, reaches a threshold where it begins to re-configure the very possibilities for production. So the question "when did it pass?" really becomes "when was that scale realized?"

It is tempting to fast forward a few centuries and date the end of the usefulness of economic theory to the first Intergovernmental Panel on Climate Change (IPCC) convened by Margaret Thatcher in 1990.[6] By that date, the scale of global pollution was already fully realized. However, the IPCC did not happen overnight. We have overshot our chronology and must rewind a bit. The IPCC lagged a growing public awareness that greenhouse gases were a threat to mankind and the biosphere. I would put the date of passage of the usefulness of economic theory twenty years earlier, around the first Earth Day: 1970. However, like the IPCC, the inaugural Earth Day also lagged another growing awareness which gelled with Rachel Carson's hugely successful *Silent Spring* in 1962. By 1966, the economist Kenneth E. Boulding expressed an alternative to mainstream theory in *The Economics of the Coming Spaceship Earth*: "The essential measure of the success of the economy is not production and consumption at all, but the nature, extent, quality, and complexity of the total capital stock, including in this the state of the human bodies and minds included in the system."[7] However, the siren for a new economics originates largely outside economics – a result consonant with Thomas Kuhn's *The Structure of Scientific Revolutions*.[8] I refer to Garrett Hardin's "The Tragedy of the Commons" and the much maligned *The Population Bomb* by Paul R. Ehrlich.[9] Both were published in 1968, the tumultuous year when students marched in Washington and on Paris. Hardin's elegantly short article quickly became one of the most cited in the history of *Science* and Ehrlich's book, an instant bestseller.[10]

The politicians of the time responded to the swelling public sentiment and the popularized scientific scholarship. In the US, the Republican administration of Richard Milhous Nixon (1968–1974) assimilated the varied lessons of the environmental movement and established the Environmental Protection Agency (EPA) in 1970. By the end of that decade, almost every country in the North had established some sort of ministry or agency of environmental protection. In the South, it took a bit longer. For example, Ecuador did not establish its Ministry of the Environment until 1996, ironically housing its temporary offices over a sales showroom for gas-guzzling four-wheel drive vehicles.

Some may disagree with my chronology of the sunk costs of economic theory and the transition to institutional limits. They will cite the Ronald Reagan counterrevolution that ushered in massive deregulation as it trumpeted unbridled capitalism. Optimism was *de rigueur* in the Reagan presidency (1980–1988) and environmentalism, the religion of Cassandras. In Reagan's mind, trees released more CO_2 than cars, and the eruption of Mount Saint Helen, more sulfur dioxide than the fleet of automobiles worldwide.[11] What the former actor did to science, he also did to economics.[12] The new "reaganomics" rested on the unlikely scenario that income tax cuts would increase tax revenue. The experiment was run over Reagan's tenure with results that were surprisingly disastrous: deficits skyrocketed to levels which were twice those predicted by the non-partisan "pessimists."[13] Although the economics profession was appalled by reaganomics, few realized how formal economic theory actually abetted it. With respect to regulation and pollution, the obtuse language of economics contrasted with the unambiguous prescriptions of "supply-side economics." Mainstream economists were viewing pollution as a technical problem awaiting a technical solution by economists tinkering with mathematical models.[14] In many ways, *The Stern Review* is both the culmination of that waiting and a rejection to wait any longer.[15]

Unlike tenured professors of economics, politicians live in the short-run and have always felt "the fierce urgency of now."[16] In the US, a succession of administrations, both Republican and Democrat (Reagan I&II, Bush-père I, Clinton I&II, and Bush-son I&II), either rescinded or refused to accept any new institutional limits proposed from abroad (e.g. the Kyoto Protocol, the Convention on Biological Diversity, the Law of the Sea). Even worse, the parties in power weakened institutional limits previously imposed from within (e.g. the standards of the Corporate Average Fuel Efficiency, the Clean Water Act, the Clean Air Act, and so on). In other words, from Reagan I through Bush-son II, vested interests succeeded in shifting costs to both the outside world and future generations of Americans. Although internal resistance existed, it was roundly ridiculed. Walter Mondale, the Democrat challenger to Reagan in the 1984 presidential race campaigned against "the credit card economy" and lost by the largest landslide ever recorded (49 of the 50 states). Success in cost-shifting reached its apogee under the brazen George W. Bush who has been labeled "conservatism's true loyal heir."[17]

And the rest of the world, where were they? Leaders in the other OECD countries were embarrassed by US excesses but not sufficiently so to say no. They kowtowed to the "Washington Consensus" which imposed austerity on the less developed countries.[18] Among other horrors, the austerity translated into reduced budgets for regulatory agencies.[19] Pusillanimity mixed with hypocrisy as one leader after another endorsed Agenda 21 – the comprehensive blueprint for *action* on sustainable development.[20] Once signed, its lofty goals were quickly forgotten. From the broad sweep of history, the Northern ecological debt to the South, which arguably began as long ago as Columbus' first voyage, assumed a new and frightening form in 1990: climate change.

Why didn't civil society in both the North and South object? The simple fact is that they did object. The most conspicuous venue has been the World Forum on Sustainable Development – the anti-Davos held annually in the South. Other actions were also noteworthy but seldom reported in the corporate news media. For the sake of space, I will mention just one. An "Ecological Debt Day" is celebrated every year and is occasionally covered by the BBC but never by the corporate media such as CNN or FOX. Ecological Debt Day is the day when humanity would have used up the resources that nature would have renewed over the entire year. The inaugural "Ecological Debt Day" was 19 December 1987 and in 2008 was moved up to 23 September. In short, the South has never slept on its rights and the legal principle of *laches* cannot be invoked.

It is easy to criticize what happened and far more difficult to construct alternatives for the future. Indeed, rejection of economic theory must mean acceptance of something else. Surprisingly, that something else is not new, not radical, and not even outside the history of economic thought. It is mainstream science and grounded in what Albert Einstein was "convinced" was "[t]he only physical theory of universal content concerning... that, within the framework of the applicability of its basic concepts, it will never be overthrown."[21] I refer to the economic implications of nineteenth century thermodynamics and more specifically, twenty-first century non-equilibrium thermodynamics (NET).

Just as economic theory is sufficiently simple to afford a thumbnail sketch, so too is NET. The first law of thermodynamics is that energy and matter are conserved. The second law, also known as the entropy law, is that disorder increases in a closed system. Apparent contradictions (e.g. life, a crystal, a flame) are in fact consistent with the second law when one recognizes that Earth's system is open and that the emerging order is at the expense of increasing disorder of the energy gradient (e.g. the food digested, the heat dissipated in crystallization, the candle wax burned). Eric Schneider, a pioneer of NET, and Dorion Sagan, a science writer, put it this way: "There are several differences between the gradient-fed cycling systems of weather and those of life. Living systems, for example, though gradient-based and cyclical, persist in the aggregate far longer than the average storm system. Nonetheless, both storm systems and those of life belong to the same class. Both are NET systems."[22]

With the public psyche prepped from the turbulent 1960s, economic theory was ready for a veritable Gestalt in the 1970s. In 1971, Nicholas Georgescu-Roegen published *The Entropy Law and the Economic Process* and in 1973, E. F. Schumacher published *Small is Beautiful: Economics as if People Mattered*. Georgescu-Roegen conceptualized resource allocation as metabolic flows of energy and material that move steadily toward the sink; Schumacher advocated appropriate technologies to manage those flows and "obtain the maximum level of well being for the minimum amount of consumption."[23] Herman E. Daly, arguably Georgescu-Roegen's most illustrious student, elaborated the implications in *Steady State Economics* (1977) and launched the operational principles of sustainable development. An identifiable school of thought had emerged but the economics profession received it with stony silence. In the preface to the second edition of *Steady State Economics* (1991), Daly writes that the first edition was "aggressively ignored by mainstream economists in major universities [even though] it did strike a responsive chord among many biologists…"[24] In the new millennium, it is far more difficult to "aggressively ignore" ecological economics as academic journals, undergraduate textbooks, and large international societies have coalesced under its banner.[25] Nevertheless, it is not impossible. *The Stern Review* does not index either ecological economics or thermodynamics and continues with economics-as-usual.

Just as economic theory affords the possibility of a simple diagram to represent resource allocation, so too does thermodynamics. However, it's the opposite of a circle. Georgescu-Roegen writes:

> [n]o other conception could be further from the correct interpretation of the facts. Even if only the physical fact of the economic process is taken into consideration, this process is not circular, but unidirectional. As far as this facet alone is concerned, the economic process consists of a continuous transformation of low entropy into high entropy, that is, into irrevocable waste or, with a topical term, into pollution.[26]

Perhaps inspired by Georgescu-Roegen, Hardin drew a unidirectional diagram for "[a] truly *general* form of the production function under the accounting rules of a society that has adopted spaceship ecology must give *equal* emphasis to *source, production,* and *sink*:

> Source (resources) → Production (alterations) → Sink (pollution thereof)"[27]

Hardin contrasted the straight line above with the "cowboy economics" of the circular process:

> *"Hazy Resources* → **Production** → *Throwaway Wastes"*[28]
> (italics and differential font size, Hardin's)

Although derisive, "cowboy" is nevertheless an apt metaphor for economists who consider resources limitless and the sink, bottomless (looking down) or infinite (looking up).[29] Metaphorically, one may even say that the 18th century Adam Smith was the first "cowboy economist" despite his never having set foot in the American West which, at the time, was Western Pennsylvania and the Ohio Valley. Smith qualifies as "cowboy" because the "invisible hand" does not recognize the physical transformation of scarce resources and its impact on the sink. Nevertheless, Smith's omission is excusable because of *scale*.[30] For example, the pin factory that Smith celebrates in Chapter One of *The Wealth of Nations* must have had a chimney to burn its coal but the smoke did not merit consideration given the vastness of the Scottish sky in 1776. But time moves on. With the industrial revolution of the 19th century, what was once an insignificant plume steadily became the Big Smoke. In the 20th century, even the sky would assume new meaning. No longer associated with any one nation, the atmosphere is now quantified by its chemical composition in parts per million (ppm) and qualified as a global commons. Thermodynamically, the atmosphere is an open access sink with a depth of barely twenty kilometers, "roughly equivalent to the skin on an apple."[31] Mainstream economists should note well that there are no substitute sinks and technology cannot create one. Those who wish to shoot our wastes into deep space, think again – the energy costs would create more entropy than the disposed wastes; those who wish to shoot our wastes into the deep Earth, think again – those cavities also have limited space.[32]

I have listened long enough to this rant, the mainstream economist will object. *Can't we extend the notions of scarcity and markets to the skin of that apple and proceed?* Brilliant minds in the profession are doing just that. They see the market as the most promising solution. Graciela Chichilnisky, UNESCO Professor of Mathematics and Economics at Columbia University, crafted the treaty language of the Kyoto Protocol without which the 60 billion dollar carbon market (and counting) in Europe would not have emerged.[33] Richard Sandor, a self-described "humble economist" who just wants "to solve the problem of global warming" has launched the voluntary Chicago Climate Exchange.[34] Other brilliant economists have also examined whether or not these new markets will have the desired effect given the complexities of international trade as well as the possibility for perverse effects.[35] Despite some reservations, the widely recognized success of tradeable permits of sulfur dioxide in the US is sufficient reason for hope for carbon markets. Nevertheless, as I will explain in the subsequent chapters, even a stunning success of tradeable emission permits can only be a bridge to the long-run solution. Using Hardin's phraseology from "The Tragedy of the Commons," the long-run solution will require "continuing education" not only because of the "human tendency to do the wrong thing" but because of an almost undetectable erosion of gains driven by an increasing population and mindless consumerism. Policymakers must multi-task and work profusely on a short-term strategy (e.g. the carbon markets, carbon taxes, and the Clean Development Mechanism) while not neglecting the long-term strategy (e.g. population policy and the formation of green preferences).[36]

The language chosen to analyze policies will channel the evolution of the simultaneous short-run and long-run policies. Although changing the wording of the Kyoto Protocol would now be a Herculean task, employing different language for its analysis is actually quite easy. *The Stern Review* uses the language of economic theory which restricts the policy options to the usual fare of permits versus taxes and combinations thereof. I will use the language of NET which, for being both discriminating and broad, renders a wider range of policy options. By talking about climate change in the terms of NET, the rationale for the Yasuní-ITT Initiative quickly comes into focus.

We may start with the term "climate change." Many of us mistakenly use the term interchangeably with "global warming," not because we do not know better, but because the latter has become fossilized in our speech through decades of repetition. On a personal note, I remember reading about global warming and the greenhouse effect in the fourth grade. That was 1965. Primary education has made great strides since the supplemental newspaper readers of the 1960s. On the "kids' page" of the Pew Center on Global Climate Change, the difference between "global warming" and "climate change" appears in one of the many FAQs: "'Global warming' refers to the increase of the Earth's average surface temperature, due to a build-up of greenhouse gases in the atmosphere. 'Climate change' is a broader term that refers to long-term changes in climate, including average temperature and precipitation."[37] On both the counts of discrimination and breadth, "climate change" is preferable to "global warming" as it allows the possibility of regional cooling as well as other climatic phenomena beyond just temperature. However, for the purposes of debate over managing the commons, "climate change" comes up short. It is sufficiently broad as to signify almost anything or nothing. Climate change lacks urgency – it carries no punch. As long ago as 500 BC, the Greek philosopher Heraclitus realized that the only thing constant is change itself: "Upon those who step into the same rivers flow other and yet other waters. All things . . . are in flux like a river."[38]

What word from NET should replace "climate change?" The answer lies in understanding the phenomenon of climate change in terms of NET. The physicist Eric J. Chaisson writes in his popular book *Cosmic Evolution: The Rise of Complexity in Nature*:

> Non-equilibrium thermodynamics stipulate that radically different states can succeed one another with sudden abruptness, an adaptation to wholly new complex states even as these *boundary conditions* slowly change. The result,

rare and catastrophic, might be violent climate change or major alteration in
surface cycling of matter and energy – a largely deterministic response to a
decidedly stochastic event, and all explainable (if not predictable) in terms of
unchanging scientific principles regarding gradients, flows, drifts, and
cycles. A common solution to the dynamical-system equations governing
non-equilibrium states...is that of a *'bifurcation.'*[39]

Despite Chaisson's choice of "climate change," the term
"fluctuation" better coheres with the adjectives "violent" and
"catastrophic." Indeed, "fluctuation" is the word that Ilya
Prigogine uses to describe such phenomena in his work on NET for
which he won the 1977 Nobel Prize in Chemistry.[40] From this
point onward, I will refer to "climate change" as "climate
fluctuations" which ultimately leads to "climate transformation."

In making the arduous adjustment to a more precise set of
terms, I am heeding the advice of E. O. Wilson that "[t]he first step
to wisdom, as the Chinese say, is getting things by their right
names."[41] From NET, climatic fluctuations are due to changes in
the atmospheric composition, (i.e. the *"boundary conditions"*),
resultant from a *"dissipation"* of underground carbon reserves into
the *"sink"* (i.e., the atmosphere). The new boundary conditions
prevent part of the infrared radiation from escaping into the other
sink (i.e. deep space). Classified thus, the issue invites a
conversation regarding access to the sink and rights over it, where
politicians, policymakers, and even "humble economists" become
"bifurcation points" with respect to future flows of energy and
matter. The terms italicized in this paragraph are again those
favored by Prigogine.

Figure 1.1 is a diagram of the greenhouse effect as it appears in
The Stern Review. Figure 1.2 is the same diagram but includes
language that is both more discriminating (the time for evolution
of the sun and the atmosphere of the Earth) while more broad
(questions regarding reclamation of the South for not having
appropriated the sink in a dirty industrialization). Because the
composition of the sink constitutes boundary conditions, the
debate post-Kyoto is a cluster of bifurcation points for the future
flows of energy and matter. One of the points in that cluster is
the Yasuní-ITT Initiative. Thinking thermodynamically, from the
bifurcation point of a novel idea can emerge amplification
effects on material and energy flows that will determine whole
systems.

Figure 1.1   The Greenhouse Effect from *The Stern Review*, 6.

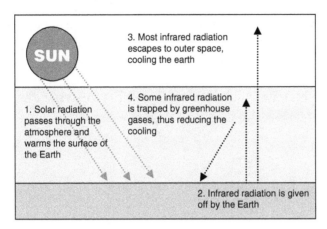

Figure 1.2   The Greenhouse Effect, Thinking Thermodynamically.

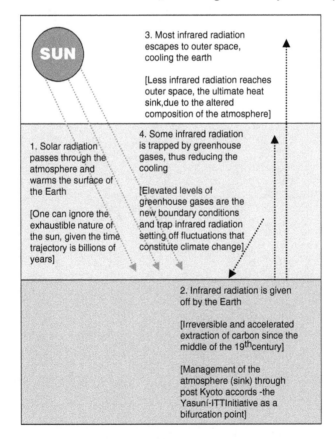

Robert L. Heilbroner would not be surprised. In the aforementioned introductory chapter of *The Worldly Philosophers*, he cites John Maynard Keynes: "The ideas of economists and political philosophers both when they are right and when they are wrong, are more powerful than is commonly understood. Indeed the world is ruled by little else...I am sure that the power of vested interests is vastly exaggerated compared with the gradual encroachment of ideas."[42]

Chapter 2

THE TRAGEDY OF THE COMMONS

A Class of Problems that has no Technical Solution

"The Tragedy of the Commons" opens with a salvo from two nuclear scientists who had thought long and deeply about the arms race between the superpowers: *"It is our considered professional judgment that this dilemma has no technical solution"* (italics in original).[1] Garrett Hardin expands upon that judgment and perceives that a whole *class* of problems exists that have no technological solution.[2] The question arises: do climate fluctuations belong to that class?

One does not need to summon the spirit of Hardin to imagine his answer. A section of "The Tragedy of the Commons" is entitled "pollution" and Hardin explains that "it is not a question of taking something out of the commons, but of putting something in...dangerous fumes in the air." What then would be Hardin's reaction to the article "Keys to Climate Protection" which opens with "Technology policy lies at the core of the climate change challenge"?[3] The author, Jeffrey D. Sachs, is arguably the world's leading development economist and the magazine, *Scientific American*, arguably the most august in American science. How would Hardin have reacted to the Sachs' short list of promising technologies? Topping that list is "Carbon Capture and Sequestration" (CCS) which "...depends on the ability to capture carbon dioxide at the power plant at low cost, transport it by pipeline over significant distances, and sequester it underground safely, reliably and durably."[4]

Again, no séance is necessary. The quote from the nuclear scientists ends with "If the great powers continue to look for solutions in the area of science and technology *only*, the result will be to worsen the situation" (italics mine).[5] In a posting to *Scientific American*, an anonymous blogger seems to have channeled the voice of Garrett Hardin:

> [C]arbon sequestering underground is fine if the amounts are small, but for the huge weights and volumes of CO_2 that must be sequestered underground for even a minor cut in the ppm levels, there will surely be geological impacts. Such storage may lead to high pressures underground and cause seismic activities, or CO_2 explosions from beneath the ground.[6]

Despite the many legitimate concerns that CCS is not "saf[e]," not "reliabl[e]," and not "durabl[e],"[7] Sachs' enthusiasm will enjoy much resonance in the public sphere.[8] The reason has more to do with religion than with rationality. "Progress-through-technology" is a "sacred cow"[9] because, as noted in the "The Tragedy" "...natural selection favors the forces of psychological denial."[10] The only role of technology for problems that have no technical solution is to facilitate "mutual coercion, mutually agreed upon." Technology buys us time as we haggle over managing the commons. However, if the time is poorly spent, then the technology will hazard an even more sudden and violent collapse.[11] Similarly, the efficiency gains wrought from technology can stimulate demand and hasten the collapse.[12] One does not have to be a sci-fi aficionado to imagine a runaway greenhouse effect for a world perched on top of a store of pressurized CO_2, sequestered *á la* Sachs over centuries.

Once we disabuse ourselves of an easy salvation through technology, we can discuss the non-technical options to manage the commons. They are:

(1) private property
(2) government regulation
(3) moral suasion and/or
(4) low human populations.

Because carbon dioxide equivalent (CO_2e) pollutants can be emitted anywhere but end up in the same sink, viz., the global atmosphere, the application of Hardin's options must be qualified as international:

(1) private property
   (tradeable emission permits through international carbon markets)
(2) government regulation
   (international carbon taxes, quotas, and/or prohibition of technologies)
(3) moral suasion
   (a global appeal to conscience and the cultivation of a green profile)
(4) low human populations
   (international policies that incorporate elements of one to three)

Among the four options, Hardin would always rank "private property" first while subordinating it and the next two to "low human populations." The supremacy of "low human populations" is grounded in the simple math of environmental impacts: an imperceptibly small growth in human populations will eventually wipe out the hard-won gains of managing the commons through (1) to (3). Even critics of "The Tragedy of the Commons" must begrudgingly recognize the levered role of population or quickly lose their credibility. For example, Anil Argawal and Sunita Narain wrote for *The New Internationalist*, on the eve of Rio'92 the Earth Summit:

> The dream of every Chinese to own a refrigerator has become the nightmare of every Northern environmentalist. The fear is that the potential for increased consumption – and therefore pollution – in the South is now the biggest threat facing the world's environment. And so hysteria has built up in the North about even the minuscule resources the South is currently using.[13]

Fast forward into the new millennium and the fear of every Northern environmentalist is no longer "hysterical" nor is the amount of resources, "minuscule."[14] In 2006, China overtook the US as the biggest CO_2 emitter.[15] Population magnifies emissions be it for relatively low consumption-high population China or through the shop-until-you-drop credo of the high consumption-relatively low population America.[16] The challenge for the Yasuní-ITT Initiative is to achieve "mutual coercion, mutually agreed upon" over management of the sink through private property and government regulation while elaborating how government can cultivate green profiles and low populations through moral suasion and positive incentives.

The *cognoscenti* of the fifteen Conferences of the Parties (COP) to the United Nations Framework Convention on Climate Change (UNFCCC) may dismay. They will object that I am embarrassingly out of the loop and do not even know the meaning of the word "sink!" Any such reaction is not nit-picking but goes to the heart of my thesis over the choice of language in framing the debate. As I will develop in the rest of this chapter, understanding the word "sink" is key to understanding why compensation for *not* extracting oil is wholly justified.

What is the meaning of "sink" in the Protocol? Although not explicitly defined, its meaning can be inferred from Article 3.3.

> The net changes in greenhouse gas emissions by sources and removals by sinks resulting from direct human-induced land-use change and forestry activities, limited to afforestation, reforestation and deforestation since 1990, measured as verifiable changes in carbon stocks in each commitment period, shall be used to meet the commitments under this Article of each Party included in Annex I. The greenhouse gas emissions by sources and removals by sinks associated with those activities shall be reported in a transparent and verifiable manner and reviewed in accordance with Articles 7 and 8.[17]

Unfortunately, an inferred meaning is inferior to an explicit definition. Fortunately, Forest Carbon Accounting, Natural Resources Canada has filled the void left by the UNFCCC and provides a useful lexicon on the web.

> Carbon sink – A carbon pool that is increasing in size. A carbon pool can be a sink for atmospheric carbon if, during a given time interval, more carbon is flowing into it than out of it

To understand that definition, one must first understand the Natural Resources Canada definition of "carbon pool":

> Carbon pool – A system having the capacity to accumulate or release carbon. Examples of carbon pools are forest biomass, wood products, soils, and the atmosphere.[18]

Examples of a "carbon sink" so defined would be any human-induced process in the carbon cycle that removes additional carbon from the atmosphere. Such meaning assigned to the word "sink" is new in the biological literature and could have been communicated by qualifying the established term "carbon pool" with words "the potential increase," viz. "the potential increase in the carbon pool."[19] Early in the "climate change" debate, climatologists did indeed put the word "sink" in quotation marks when referring to the potential increase in the carbon pool.[20] One can interpret the quotation marks as a sign of discomfort, no doubt because "sink" is a well known term from thermodynamics and "climate change" is a thermodynamic phenomenon. Despite the importance of the Kyoto Protocol, many ecologists have correctly not switched the meaning of "sink." As recently as 2008, Paul R. and Anne H. Ehrlich write "The atmospheric sink in which CO_2 and other products of fossil fuel energy use are deposited is a classic open access resource..."[21]

Definitions matter. A lawyer probably needs no persuasion of the truth of that statement but the economist does. To the economist, debates over definitions are often disparaged as frivolous. Ever since Paul Samuelson published *Foundations of Economic Analysis*,[22] economists have celebrated math as the language of economics and ignored the role of rhetoric in resource allocation.[23] So, I ask mainstream economists who work on "climate change": is income growth (dY/dt), "the income sink"? Is capital accumulation (dK/dt), "the capital sink"? When the carbon-rich South wishes to claim compensation for the Northern appropriation of the atmospheric "sink," audiences in both the North and South will easily misinterpret the claim. The audience will equivocate on the inferred meaning of "carbon sink" from the Kyoto Protocol and start talking about new absorption of CO_2 through human-induced land use changes in forests and soils.[24] To compound the confusion, the South would indeed like to be compensated for human induced increases in the carbon pool but that is a separate issue. First, the South would like to be compensated for the appropriation of the atmospheric sink into which the North has "pu[t] something in...[viz.,] dangerous fumes." The Kyoto Protocol has switched the discussion over the "sink" by implying a new meaning to that word and thereby undermined the much needed debate over appropriation.

Like "climate change" in Chapter One and "carbon sink" here, other terms in the Kyoto Protocol are also problematic. For example, the Parties talk about carbon being "sequestered" while the biological literature refers to carbon *dioxide* being "fixed" in the carbon cycle. The use of "carbon sequestration" has a subtle disadvantage that will escape mono-lingual English speakers. The cognates of "sequester" in the romance languages mean "abduction." In the context of CO_2, the Spanish phrase *secuestro de carbono* or the more stilted *secuestración de carbono* is comical. The translation creates undue levity over something which is deadly serious. *Fijación de dioxido de carbono* or *captura de carbono* causes no such distraction. Why don't policymakers use the correct terms from ecology?

Garrett Hardin offered an answer in his deliciously wicked *Exploring New Ethics for Survival: The Voyage of the Spaceship Beagle*.[25] Chapter 8 is entitled "Word Magic" and I quote the first two sentences and then jump to the closing phrases. When the quotes are read with "climate change" in mind, one begins to understand how policy-makers control the debate by controlling the language:

> The official function of language is to facilitate thought and communication. One of its unofficial functions, just as real, is to *prevent* thought and communication... Development? Not on your life. *Destruction. Defacement...* "Development" is word magic, designed to keep us from thinking...(italics, Hardin's).[26]

In the first chapter, I argue that "climate fluctuations" is preferable to "climate change" and in this chapter, "potential increase in the carbon pool," preferable to "carbon sink," and "carbon dioxide fixation," to "carbon sequestration." My insistence over precision in language is neither fetish nor fastidiousness. Only the first term in each of the pairs integrates easily with non-equilibrium thermodynamics (NET) and only NET provides an integrating framework for how structures irreversibly dissipate energy flows toward the sink which was appropriated by the North. The accusation of appropriation is not about the emissions that began in England with mid-nineteenth century industrialization, even though the economics profession already had an idea about the implications of thermodynamics.[27] The accusation is based on the expansion of emissions since 1990 when the first IPCC put the issue beyond reasonable doubt that the industrialized countries would have to cut their emissions by 60%.[28] By 2004, emissions had gone *up* 49% in Spain, 16% in the US, and 7% in Japan while they have gone *down* 17% in Germany, 1.1% in Denmark, and 14% in the UK[29] *Ergo*, all of the aforementioned industrialized countries increased their carbon debt, some more so than others.

For any claim there must be remedy, and just as one must justify the claim, one must also justify the remedy. What remedy would right the wrong and also cohere with management of the atmospheric sink? Whereas the NET framework makes sense of the claim by examining the appropriation of the sink since 1990, the NET framework does not as easily generate implications for the remedy. Economic theory does. Over the last half of the twentieth century, economic theory has painstakingly fleshed out the implications of optimization. Amazingly, the language from that theory has not been deployed in the UNFCCC dialog to identify the phenomenon that would justify the remedy. I refer to the word "leakage."

Neither the Protocol or Natural Resources Canada defines "leakage" but definitions do exist. A precise one can be found by Tom Manders and Hans Timmer from the Netherlands Bureau for Economic Policy Analysis: "Carbon leakage is the endogenous increase in carbon emissions as a result of emission reductions elsewhere."[30] The definition lends itself to data collection and analysis. For example, the economist Sergey V. Paltsev, elaborates a pollution-haven hypothesis where "[c]arbon emission abatement in a group of countries can result in increased emissions in non-abating countries. This effect has been referred to as carbon leakage. The Kyoto Protocol calls for a number of industrialized countries to limit their emissions while other countries have no abatement commitments."[31] However, "leakage" is a phenomenon that is broader than just the decision as to where to locate polluting factories. A distinct context appears in Chapter 25 of *The Stern Review*, "Reversing Emissions from Land Use Change," where Stern recognizes the "substantial risk that, if small areas are protected, leakage to other areas could take place and overall emissions would not be reduced."[32] Stern cites Nobel Memorial Laureate[33] Joseph Stiglitz that "the combination of existing incentives in place to plant new forests, but no or insufficient incentives to preserve existing forests, could encourage perverse behavior with forests being cut down, and then replanted."[34] Although both pollution havens and perverse incentives are the economic deductions of the Kyoto Protocol, the term "leakage" does not easily integrate the two nor does it suggest any policy implication.

The choice of the word "leakage" by economists is bizarre because a precise term exists within economic theory that would integrate the two phenomena and also suggest policy implications. I refer to the word "distortion" as used in the "General Theory of Second Best" by Richard Lipsey and Kelvin Lancaster, published in *The Review of Economic Studies* in 1956. Put simply, the theory of second best means that removing one distortion can actually make the economy more *inefficient* when related distortions are left in place. So, internalizing the costs of CO_2 emissions in one country could cause industry flight to another country that has no such commitment (pollution haven). The asymmetry is a distortion, not a "leakage." Similarly, paying to increase the carbon pool through planting trees may cause landowners to burn the standing trees because they do not have to pay for the CO_2 emissions of the scorched land. The asymmetry is a distortion, not a "leakage." By using the correct economic term, we see that pollution havens and perverse effects are simply different expressions of the theory of second best.

Second best is devastating for policy based on piecemeal removal of distortions which may explain why it does not get incorporated into introductory textbooks.[35] However, correct language can do more than simply group seemingly disparate phenomena. One implication of second best is that when a distortion cannot be removed, adding another may make the system more *efficient*. That implication is devastating for textbook economics and gets omitted edition after edition. In "Reflections on the General Theory of Second Best on its Golden Jubilee," Lipsey considers "the allegation that second best theory provides justification for just about any crazy interventionist policy."[36] His elegant response to the cognitive dissonance of mainstream economists is apropos for *The Economics of the Yasuní Initiative*:

> Highly elaborate theory is not necessary in these cases and many others like them. What is needed is a good appreciative understanding of how the price system works, as well as understanding the cautionary warning from second best theory that any policy may have unexpected and undesirable consequences in apparently unrelated parts of the economy that need to be watched for and mitigated where necessary. Useful piecemeal policy advising is not impossible; neither can it be determined purely

scientifically; instead it is an art, assisted by good economics, both theoretical and empirical.[37]

For the Yasuní-ITT Initiative, the relevancy of second best is clear. Ecuador and many other carbon-rich countries in the South are not restrained by any "cap" of CO_2 emissions in the "cap and trade" of Kyoto. They are the non-Annex ratified Parties to the Kyoto Protocol. Their absence in Annex I is a "distortion" in the economic policy of "internalization of externalities" through "cap and trade." The distortion cannot be easily dismounted given the fact that no wealthy country ever became developed without a dirty industrialization. Poverty levels in Ecuador in 1997, when the Kyoto Protocol was signed, had reached almost half the population. In the absence of an effective "cap," Ecuador and other carbon-rich non-Annex I countries will extract their petroleum. Whenever they sell it to other countries which also do not have a "cap," they increase the CO_2 in the atmospheric sink. By the theory of second best, one can justify payment to Ecuador for not extracting its petroleum and preventing the future release of CO_2 into the global commons. A more detailed explanation of second best and the Yasuní-ITT Initiative is elaborated in Chapter 4. I mention it here briefly because it dovetails with the requisite discussion about justifying the claim as well as the remedy.

In the early 1990s, I contemplated the likely international conversation about carbon markets and foresaw that "the shrillest cries of unfairness will be from the fossil-fuel-rich countries...Imagine that China, with its 300-year supply of coal deposits, demands to be paid not to pursue a coal-fueled industrialization. Such an argument has no ethical foundation. It is the moral equivalent of blackmail. 'Pay us not to take us both into the greenhouse world.'"[38] The argument extends to standing forests and underground petroleum reserves. Have I changed my mind? At the time I originally wrote those lines (1992), the entry in the ecological debt for climate fluctuation was just starting to tick.[39] Only with the issuance of the IPCC report in 1990 did the world have evidence, beyond reasonable doubt, that climate fluctuations were indeed anthropogenic. As Hardin quotes from *Situation Ethics* "*the morality of an act is a function of the state of the system at the time it is performed.*"[40] Until 1990, the North could make the case that the jury was still out and the Southern claim, akin to blackmail. In light of the IPCC released in 1990, they should have begun the cuts. Because no wealthy industrialized country achieved the recommended 60% reduction, the claim, which once lacked moral justification, has now become totally justified.

The reception to the argument above will depend largely on the ethics of the audience. For those schooled in cowboy Economics 101 and never advanced to graduate courses and the theory of second best, it will feel wrong to pay someone something for doing nothing. Nevertheless, the possibility of persuasion is not hopeless. Ethics is not just nurture but also nature. The etiology of fairness is well expressed by *The New York Times* columnist David Brooks "Most of us make snap moral judgments about what feels fair or not, or what feels good or not. We start doing this when we are babies, before we have language. And even as adults, we often can't explain to ourselves why something feels wrong."[41] For audiences schooled with some understanding of thermodynamics, it will feel right to pay for what their country appropriated, viz., a disproportionate share of the sink. Knowledge of the rudimentary physics will allow such audiences to express a fairness that is innate to mankind and the other primates.[42] Largely for that reason, I have subtitled this book "Climate Change as if Thermodynamics Mattered."

Now that we have scratched the surface of the answer to "Why should the international community pay anyone for doing nothing?" we should proceed to the next two questions raised in the closing of the Introduction. "What should they pay?" and "how would they pay it?" Although the answers are the themes for Chapters 3 and 5, I will broach the questions here as they belong to a class of problem that has no technical solution. In other words, they too require an international conversation about what feels "fair."

Rafael Correa expressed his support for the Yasuní-ITT Initiative in a language that resonates with fairness. His words were accompanied by action. On the 30th of March 2007, Correa froze the bidding scheduled by PetroEcuador for the Yasuni-ITT fields with these words:

> Leaving the crude underground is accepted as preferable in order not to affect an area of extraordinary biodiversity and not risk the existence of several communities in voluntary isolation or without contact. The measure will be fully taken into consideration as long as the international community compensates for at least half the resources that would have been obtained from petroleum extraction - resources that the Ecuadorian economy requires for its development [translation mine].[43]

The intended audience of the passage was both national and international. A goal of *The Economics of the Yasuní Initiative* is to show that the national and the international justifications for the Yasuní-ITT Initiative are not only complementary but also mutually reinforcing. In the beginning of this chapter, I justified the Yasuní-ITT Initiative by highlighting how Northern countries have appropriated the atmospheric sink at the expense of Southern countries. I also justified compensation for *not* extracting oil by the theory of second best. Now I must make the vision operational both nationally and internationally. The passage above becomes a mixed bag on a few critical points.

1. Laudably, it recognizes the existence value of biodiversity and the right of the Tagaere and Taromenane communities to live in voluntary isolation. Regrettably, it assumes that such rights hold no primacy when, under national and international law, they very well may. Nevertheless, the widespread poverty of Ecuador softens the accusations of violation of human rights because *"the morality of an act is a function of the state of the system at the time it is performed."*[44]

2. Laudably, it requires that "the international community" which benefits from biodiversity conservation pay for the opportunity costs of that conservation. Regrettably, it fails to discriminate the variance among those who benefit. Nevertheless, the tacit assumption is that we are speaking about the G-8 countries.[45]

3. Laudably, it sets an amount, "half the resources that would have been forthcoming from petroleum extraction." Regrettably, it implies that the calculation of that value is within our lens of resolution. Nevertheless, the parameter of "half" is appealing as 50-50 deals are usually the easiest to consummate.[46]

4. Laudably, it recognizes that development requires capital investment. Regrettably it does not tell us how much capital will be required for development or when the world will know that Ecuador has achieved the status of a developed nation. Nevertheless, indicators exist to measure development.

Of all these misgivings, the most troubling is the calculation of value. The original estimate of the compensation was quoted in the international press at \$350 million annually for ten years.[47] That annuity implies that someone did a discounted cost-benefit analysis of recoverable crude petroleum over the lifetime of the ITT oil fields. Any economist should cringe. The equilibrium price of crude is a moving target that rises (+) or falls (–) by increasing or decreasing demand and falls (–) or rises (+) by increasing or decreasing supply. To get a flavor for how difficult is any such calculation, consider the following overview.

On the demand side, the economist would have to estimate, among other things, the impacts of:

(1) the globalization of industrialization using carbon technologies (+),
(2) the substitution of industrial processes using renewable energies (–),
(3) the changes in incomes and disparities of incomes (+ or –) as well as
(4) war or peace in one the most volatile parts of the world (+ or –).

On the supply side, the economist would have to estimate, among other things:

(1) the worldwide discovery of new reserves (–),
(2) the worldwide exhaustion of old reserves (+),
(3) innovation of new technologies to extract reserves (–) and again
(4) war or peace (– or +).

Once all these estimates are made, one would then have to choose the appropriate discount rate which is a subject of endless debate in the profession. If all this were not daunting enough, he or she or they (i.e. the team of economists) would then have to estimate the price elasticities of both supply and demand, viz., the responsiveness of demand and supply to a carbon tax and/or the internalized costs of a cap and trade mechanism. This last point requires a bit more explanation. If demand is price inelastic and supply elastic, then the incidence of the carbon tax will fall largely on the consumer; if the reverse is true, then it falls on the supplier.

If I or any other academic economist knew the answers to the aforementioned questions, we would probably be enjoying early retirement on the sunny French Riviera. Knowing how to speculate in future markets is what made George Soros a multi-billionaire. The nature of a coherent policy framework cannot rest on speculation of the future price of petroleum. The inevitable disagreement over predictions (too high? too low? just right?) will derail the necessary debate over what is a fair remedy for the North having appropriated the sink since 1990.

Despite all the misgivings, one can say that Correa is correct. Ecuador requires capital to develop. From the viewpoint of the long sweep of history, Ecuador is in a bottleneck between two economies, that of the cowboy and that of the spaceship. E. O. Wilson puts it this way "[W]e have entered the Century of the Environment, in which the immediate future is usefully conceived as a bottleneck. Science and technology, combined with a lack of self-understanding and a Paleolithic obstinacy, brought us to where we are today. Now science and technology, combined with foresight and moral courage, must see us through the bottleneck and out."[48]

The next three chapters will elaborate how the compensation for not extracting the oil should be the dollar amount for the infrastructure that would have been invested in exploration of the ITT oil fields. Unlike predictions over the price of petroleum over the next ten years, the amount of investment and operational costs forgone over the next four years can be calculated with few misgivings. It has been estimated at approximately $5 billion.[49] The substitute investment should be an array of projects that promote sustainability and is the theme of Chapter 5. Who should pay *within* the North for that investment is the theme of Chapter 3.

The skeptic will fear that Ecuador will take the money now and drill later. For this reason, the guarantee designed into the Yasuní-ITT Initiative will help keep the incentives aligned should the political pendulum swing and some future government repudiate the commitments made by the Correa government. The lien allows international claims to cloud the importation of Ecuadorian crude should a retrograde government rescind on the commitment to leave the oil underground. As is well known, oil is highly fungible and can find its way to ports that also flout the claims. It could also be used internally. The guarantee is the stick in the proverbial carrot-and-stick of incentives.

What is the carrot for the future governments of Ecuador? The answer must come from a post-Kyoto accord in which Ecuador is compensated for having avoided CO_2 emissions in year five and beyond. How much? Again, the French Riviera beckons. The value will vary with the carbon market. If 40 million tons of carbon is avoided in year five, and the price is at an historic low of $1 per metric ton, then the payment will be only $40 million. If it is the historic high of $30, then it will be $1.2 billion. The important point is this: at any moment that Ecuador re-opens bidding on the ITT oil fields, the carrot is abruptly withdrawn and the stick, brandished.

The sentence above seems to imply that Ecuador will receive payments *ad infinitum* as long as it does not drill. How fair is that? We must focus on the last part of Point #4 on page 23 above. At some future date Ecuador will have passed through Wilson's bottleneck and the justification for the claim will no longer hold. Fortunately, a precedent exists. Even without having achieved a truly sustainable economy, Costa Rica relinquished the possibility of petroleum extraction in 2001. The then newly elected president placed a moratorium on offshore exploration and asked for no compensation in exchange. The commitment was quickly put to the test. Harken Energy of Texas sued, demanding $57 billion in damages. Costa Rica stood fast and the suit was dropped.[50] When Ecuador can boast the status of "High Human Development" in the UNDP Human Development Index as can Costa Rica since 2002,[51] then one can say that Ecuador has passed through the bottleneck and payments can stop for avoided CO_2 emissions.

Chapter 3

THE WILLFUL IGNORANCE OF *REALPOLITIK*

Market Failure or Cost-Shifting Success?

Nineteen Eighty-Four should be required reading for anyone who votes. Through a tale of totalitarian dystopia, George Orwell shows how the State can distort language for its ever shifting purposes. "Doublespeak" is one of the neologisms of the novel that has entered the vernacular.[1] What exactly is it? According to William Lutz, professor of English:

> Doublespeak is a language which pretends to communicate but really doesn't. It is language which makes the bad seem good, the negative appear positive, the unpleasant appear attractive, or at least tolerable. It is language which avoids or shifts responsibility, language which is at variance with its real or purported meaning. It is language which conceals or prevents thought. Doublespeak is the language which does not extend thought but limits it.[2]

Despite the gravity of the phenomenon, humorous examples abound. For example, *The Quarterly Journal of Doublespeak* reports a vote by the Minnesota Board of Education "...to consider requiring all students do some 'volunteer work' as a prerequisite for High School graduation."[3] We can all laugh. But there is nothing laughable when, say, the US government refers to the drowning of prisoners denied *habeas corpus* as the "waterboarding" of "detainees." Doctors were on duty to perform tracheotomies if necessary.[4]

In the spectrum of doublespeak, I am tempted to locate the "market failure" of economic theory somewhere between the "volunteer work" mandated by the Minnesota Board of Education and the "waterboards" authorized in the Bush Administration Torture Memos. But I resist the temptation. Due to the number of victims from climate fluctuations, "market failure" lies far to the right of "waterboards." I base my assessment on *The Stern Review* which makes abundantly clear that "the estimates of damage could rise to 20% of GDP or more."[5] Trillions of dollars of avoidable damages translate into millions of avoidable deaths even though most of the victims will be invisible. For example, a death from an inadequate sanitation infrastructure does not lend itself to photography as does a corpse floating face down in the aftermath of a hurricane. The reader may stop and wonder: where is the connection between "market failure" and such avoidable deaths? To answer that question, we must examine the meaning of "market failure" and how that meaning demonstrates a willful ignorance of *realpolitik*.[6]

The Stern Review is the node in any such economic discussion. Section 2.2 is entitled "Understanding the market failures that lead to climate change" and the opening sentence sets the stage. "In common with many other environmental problems, human-induced climate change is at its most basic level an externality."[7] That statement is wrong. Human-induced "climate change" is at its most basic level a physical phenomenon. To repeat the thumbnail sketch of Chapter 1, the atmosphere is a sink and changes in its boundary conditions, viz., CO_2e, may result in violent fluctuations. Upon the wrong premise that "climate change" is irreducible beyond "externality," Stern continues "[t]hose who produce greenhouse-gas emissions are bringing about climate change, thereby imposing costs on the world and on future generations..."[8] The assertion implies that once society realizes "the full consequences of the costs of [the] actions of [those who impose costs]," corrective policies will ensue.

The experiment has been run. For a least a half century, "market failure" has been a core concept in economics as evidenced by its prominence in introductory textbooks. Sixteen years have lapsed from the time that the IPCC issued its first report and Stern's draft of Section 2.2. Over all those years, neoliberal governments throughout the North did not make operational the economic theory to which they supposedly subscribed. As mentioned in Chapter 2, no country took sufficient measures to cut back emissions by the IPCC recommended 60% and some countries let the emissions significantly rise. As a core concept in economics, "market failure" failed miserably to persuade governments about what to do. Nevertheless, Stern maintains that "[climate change] must be regarded as market failure on the greatest scale the world has seen."[9]

The *sine qua non* of science is falsifiability.[10] As one contemplates Stern's remarks, one begins to understand that the usefulness of "market failure" is not falsifiable. If pollution policies are corrected in light of the concept of "market failure," through carbon taxes and/or "cap and trade," then the concept is indeed a useful one. If pollution policies are *not* corrected in the light of "market failure," then the concept is simply not useful. As Stern's quote makes clear, pollution policies have *not* been corrected as "[climate change] must be regarded as market failure on the greatest scale the world has seen." However, Stern finds its abject failure as evidence of its future usefulness! Karl Popper would spin.

Market failure "avoids or shifts responsibility" and qualifies as doublespeak. To address or assign responsibility, the concept should be replaced with "cost-shifting success," a term coined by Martin O'Connor and Joan Martinez-Alier who are pioneers in ecological economics.[11] Via some simple word substitutions, "climate [fluctuations] must be regarded as [cost-shifting success] on the greatest scale the world has seen." Although the substitutions in the prior sentence "would extend thought rather than limit it," ecological economists will never be able to persuade the mainstream economist. The language of resource allocation is simply not open for discussion. Stern writes "The basic theory of externalities and public goods is the starting point for most economic analyses of climate change and this Review is no exception."[12] Knowing the futility of arguing with mainstream economists, the ecological economist must make an end run to the public. Joan Martinez-Alier has done just that in a response letter to *The Economist* regarding their coverage of the Yasuní-ITT Initiative. He takes exception to the use of "market failure" and introduces "cost-shifting success" to millions of readers.[13]

Any public conversation that discusses "cost-shifting success" recognizes implicitly the *realpolitik* of resource allocation. Cost-shifting success implies that the "supply" in "supply and demand" will subvert pollution policy just as it has long manipulated "demand" through advertising. The approach dovetails with the lifetime work of John Kenneth Galbraith (1908–2006) and his intellectual descendants. To counter the heavy hand of corporate influence, Galbraith suggested that the university, in concert with trade unions, assume the role of "countervailing power."[14] Alas, the suggestion now seems hopelessly outdated. In the new millennium, titles such as *How the University Works: Higher Education and the Low Wage Nation* and *The Last Professors: The Corporate University and the Fate of the Humanities* signal the sorry state of academic affairs.[15] Nevertheless, all is not gloom. A few accomplished scholars have ventured outside the ivory tower *á la* Galbraith and spoken unabashedly about the *realpolitik* of resource allocation. One thinks of the weekly columns in *The New York Times* by the 2008 Nobel Memorial Prize Laureate in Economics Paul Krugman or the award winning books of the polymath Jared Diamond. To broadly educated readers, Krugman explains "crony capitalism"[16] and Diamond, the logic of "kleptocracies."[17] Unfortunately, their arguments will not convince anyone who purposefully does *not* read anything written by Krugman or Diamond.

Why, pray tell, would anyone who isn't a crony capitalist or an obliging kleptocrat remain willfully ignorant about crony capitalism or kleptocracy? Thorstein Veblen solved the conundrum over a century ago. The victims are bound up in the ideology of the aggressors and want to *emulate* them.[18] Rephrasing Karl Marx, they have nothing to lose but their delusions which, unfortunately, they cherish.

Recognition of the *realpolitik* of climate fluctuations means that one must change the culture of the audiences. It is a tall order but not an impossible one. Critical thinking must be celebrated and science becomes key. Scientists enjoy a certain reputation for neutrality as well as innate intelligence and mental discipline. To the extent the population is scientifically uneducated, popularization of science is a necessity. Scientists must become the Galbraithian "countervailing power." Unfortunately, *realpolitik* means that the corporate media will counter that "countervailing power." The scientist will quickly be portrayed as a Cassandra, an opportunist, and/or an egghead. A perfect storm arises when the academic peers of the scientist sneer at his or her successful popularization, with an intensity in proportion to the scholar's popular success.[19] Not surprisingly, there are few scientific popularizers despite a pent-up demand. The mainstream economist may see in what I have just written "market failure" – perhaps "academic failure" – but I would call it more accurately "inhibition by corporate harassment and professional envy." So, a niche opens for any non-academic non-scientist who has a gift for communication and the wherewithal to do battle. Again, the corporate interests do not stand idle. They shift tactics. Now challenging a non-academic non-scientist, the corporate media will substitute the "egghead" epithet for that of "dupe of junk science."

Enter Al Gore. His *An Inconvenient Truth* is a heartfelt personal journey with a narrative style that is highly unconventional. It is anything but the work of an egghead. The subtitle *The Planetary Emergency of Global Warming and What We Can Do About It* projects and then dispels the epithet of Gore as Cassandra.[20] We are given solid scientific evidence as to the planetary emergency in the first 304 pages followed by twenty three pages of what we can do. Obviously Gore is not a Cassandra, not an egghead, and not a dupe. The only label which retains some traction is that of "opportunist." Indeed, within memory Gore campaigned twice for the highest office of the most powerful country in the world. Is *An Inconvenient Truth* his platform for a third attempt? Gore looks that Gorgon in the face, "So whether you are a Democrat or a Republican, whether you voted for me or not, I very much hope that you will sense that my goal is to share with you both my passion for the Earth and my deep sense of concern for its fate."[21]

Tellingly, *An Inconvenient Truth* is not mentioned once in the *The Stern Review*, even though it debuted to high acclaim five months prior to the first printing of *The Stern Review*. This *lacuna* should be cause for self-evaluation of every mainstream economist. Why should the themes of *An Inconvenient Truth* – the persistence of denial, the necessity of political engagement, and the possibility of behavior modification – lie beyond the domain of economic theory?

Gore uses science adroitly. His *modus operandi* is reminiscent of Garrett Hardin: engage the public in a discussion about a problem that has no purely technical solution, viz., climate fluctuations, and then seek "mutual coercion, mutually agreed upon," *inter alia*, the

Kyoto Protocol.[22] An incredible number of examples can be found that support my interpretation. I will cite just a few, beginning with the statistics of corporate disinformation about global warming. The numbers are reported in extra large typeface: 928 relevant articles appeared in scientific journals over a ten year period and none expressed doubt as to the cause, while 636 articles in the popular press over a fourteen period, 53% expressed such doubt.[23] Gore then elaborates the mechanics behind the statistics:

> At the beginning of 2001, President Bush hired a lawyer/lobbyist named Phillip Cooney to be in charge of environmental policy in the White House. For the previous six years, Cooney had worked at the American Petroleum Institute and was the person principally in charge of the oil and coal companies' campaign to confuse the American people about this issue. Even though Cooney has no scientific training whatsoever, he was empowered by the president to edit and censor the official assessments of global warming from the EPA and other parts of the federal government.[24]

Because seeing is believing, Cooney's marked-up passage from *The New York Times* to the president is reproduced in the lower corner of the page.

My discussion of design and imagery is not peripheral to the *realpolitik* of resource allocation nor to the overarching framework of non-equilibrium thermodynamics. Human vision evolved to dissipate the energy gradients of the African savannahs. Our minds are adapted not only to look at images but also make "moral snap judgments" based on the images seen. For example, *An Inconvenient Truth* has a two page photograph of a farm worker burning rainforest to clear land for ranching in Rondônia, Brazil.[25] Contrast the reader's reception to that image with the reception to the bar diagrams of global land use changes in *The Stern Review*.[26] Granted an egghead may prefer the bar diagrams but the real question is whether or not those diagrams evoke any reflection about the ethics of the burning and living within limits. Even for the egghead, I am sure the diagrams do not. Brilliantly, Gore realizes that the most effective rhetoric to discuss limits is a combination of science and art.

Another comparison reading drives home my point. In *An Inconvenient Truth*, the collapse of coral reefs is projected through a photograph of the blue-green lettuce coral of the Phoenix Islands, Kiribati, Polynesia, followed by the bleached coral in the Rongelap

Reef, Marshall Islands. The discerning reader sees that the fish in the latter photograph are absent.[27] For the egghead who dismisses the photographs as anecdotal, Gore includes a map of the world with optimal coral habitat in different colors shown for the pre-industrial (1880), current (2000) and near-future (2050) worlds. By 2050, there is no optimal or adequate habitat left, just the marginal or extremely low. Now consider the treatment of same phenomenon in *The Stern Review*. One sentence appears on page 93, "Coral bleaching has become increasingly prevalent since the 1980s," and a couple more sentences are relegated to a textbox about Australia on page 147. Lost to the reader of *The Stern Review* is any indignation for the eradication of coral reefs worldwide, analogous on many levels to having eradicated all the tropical rainforests of the world in one full swoop.

An Inconvenient Truth is a visual banquet from beginning to end whose visual richness is evidenced by two full pages of closing credits in typeset 8. *The Stern Review* sports just one photo in the entire book and it appears on the cover: the planet Earth stripped of cloud cover on which night has fallen in the Western Hemisphere. Nevertheless, Stern should be congratulated for the selection. The image embodies the perspicacity of American surrealist painter Georgia O'Keefe "Nothing is less real than realism. It is only by selection, by eliminating, by emphasis that we get at the real meanings of things."[28] The clustered distribution of artificial lights is in direct proportion to population density and affluence. Looking at the bright clusters in North America and Western Europe, there is little doubt as to the causes. In contrast but with equal merit, is the image on Gore's front cover of *An Inconvenient Truth*: the blue planet enshrouded with the stuff of NET – whorls of clouds.

The adept use of imagery epitomizes the conviction that that no technical solution exists to the problem of climate fluctuations. Audiences must be engaged to open the books and read. Sadly, most people will never be convinced to open any book and read anything. Better than photographs and text are moving pictures and an engaging script. In the Introduction, Gore writes

My principal concern in [the proposition of a film] was that the translation of the slide show into a film not sacrifice the central role of science for entertainment's sake…I talked with this extraordinary group, and felt their deep commitment to exactly the same goals I was pursuing, the more convinced I became that the movie was a good idea. If I wanted to reach the maximum number of people quickly, and not just continue talking to a few hundred people a night, a movie was the way to do it.[29]

Gore's pictures, either moving in the documentary or still in the book, integrate into the narrative just as Hardin recommended in "The Tragedy."

In passing, it is worth noting that the morality of an act cannot be determined from a photograph. One does not know whether a man killing an elephant or setting fire to the grassland is harming others until one knows the total system in which his act appears. 'One picture is worth a thousand words,' said an ancient Chinese; but it may take ten thousand words to validate it. It is as tempting to ecologists as it is to reformers in general to try to persuade others by way of the photographic shortcut. But the essence of an argument cannot be photographed: it must be presented rationally – in words.[30]

What Hardin missed but Gore perceived is the role of photography in helping us overcome denial. Photographs counteract what Hardin described as "the natural tendency to do the wrong thing."[31] It is no coincidence that Holocaust museums around the world rely heavily on photography. The images of victims, no matter how painful to see, help us define our ethics.

Some of the imagery in *An Inconvenient Truth* shows just how unoriginal is the thesis of corporate media campaigns and public harm. For example, opposite the statistics on media bias in the reporting of global warming, Gore reproduces a 1950s advertisement from R. J. Reynolds Tobacco Co. "More Doctors Smoke Camels than any other cigarette!"[32] For a half century, outstanding public intellectuals exposed just such disinformation. In 1995, Sagan wrote:

When the first work was published in the scientific literature in 1953 showing that the substances in cigarette smoke when painted on the backs of rodents produce malignancies, the response of the six major tobacco companies was to initiate a public relations campaign to impugn the research, sponsored by the Sloan Kettering Foundation. This is similar to what the Du Pont Corporation did when the first research was published in 1974 showing that their Freon product attacks the protective ozone layer. There are many other examples.[33]

In reminding us of *realpolitik* through images and text, we inevitably return to the question of fairness, be it for the flight attendant who succumbs to second hand smoke or for the Polynesian who will lose both his home and his homeland to climate fluctuations. Undoubtedly, such talk will turn off the economist accustomed to paying only lip service to fairness. Although efficiency and equity are introduced early in any textbook on the principles of economics, the concepts are always about "efficiency and *equity*" (to borrow Hardin's typographic technique). The tactic is similar to the talk about products in the circular flow diagrams of introductory textbooks and then, a few pages later, the pesky issue of externalities.

In order to brook a discussion about climate fluctuations and fairness with economists, one must distinguish the contexts of the typical accusations of unfairness. Two distinct scenarios are easily conflated. The standard one is a transaction where two parties freely exercise their willingness to buy or sell in the marketplace. Should one of the parties later feel him/herself the loser, the economist reasons, he/she should not have consummated the transaction in the first instance but bought or sold elsewhere. In such televised debates, Milton Friedman would interject *caveat emptor* triumphantly.[34] Let the buyer beware! There is much merit in the disdain for the cries of unfairness in such scenarios. But the unfairness argument over the atmospheric sink is fundamentally different. The South agreed to nothing when the North polluted the planet pell-mell. Perhaps realizing this, the North has quickly changed the storyline. Today it runs something like this: the atmosphere was wrongly perceived as resilient until scientists demonstrated that a limit had indeed been overshot at which time management of the global commons became justified. That storyline is unobjectionable as long as it is accompanied by a timeline. If the perception of resilience is dated later than 1990, i.e., after the issuance of the first IPCC, then the story is fraudulent. It is a convenient falsehood to an inconvenient truth. Perceiving the fraud, the South will not and should not abandon its demand for compensation. Should their claim fall on deaf ears, the carbon-rich countries of the South will experience, rightly or wrongly, few qualms in industrial development in the same dirty fashion as has the North. With a sense of irony, they may even recycle the same storyline that the science of climate fluctuations is not yet conclusive. Remembering that they signed on to the UNFCCC, they could alternatively point to their poverty and cite Garrett Hardin *"the morality of an act is a function of the state of the system at the time it is performed."*[35]

Unless the issue of fairness is resolved for the carbon-rich countries of the South, the tragedy of the commons will ensue, hazarding the possibility of a runaway greenhouse effect.

To get a carbon rich country through the bottleneck from a cowboy economy to that of a spaceship, the question remains. Who should pay? Anyone affiliated with state-run universities in Latin America knows the answer by heart. The May Day placard reads, *La crisis ¡que la paguen los ricos!* ("The crisis – let the rich pay!"). We now hear the spirit of Milton Friedman chortling…*Who are these rich? Did they incur the costs that must now be borne?* If the rich incurred the costs, then they should pay. But the ethics of having to pay when one did not incur the costs is more ambiguous. For example, the rich pay taxes destined for public university education or transfer payments for mothers with dependent children even though many will never access either government program.

Whatever merit exists in the perennial complaints by the rich, they vanish with respect to greenhouse gas. Climate fluctuations is the best example to justify *La crisis ¡que la paguen los ricos!* Through over-consumption, the economically rich have indeed caused the crisis and should now pay to help the carbon-rich but economically poor countries through the bottleneck. Such accountability is fairly obvious and obviously fair.

The question nags. Who are "the rich?" They certainly must not be equated with "rich countries" as poverty levels in the richest country in the world, the US, account for 12% of the population with some 58% qualifying as poor sometime in their lives between ages 25 and 75.[36] But statistics are mind-numbing and pale against a quick YouTube search of "tent cities" and "California," arguably America's richest state. Should austerity be imposed on the inhabitants of these "Bush Gardens?"[37] Many in the South would mercilessly say yes – an eye for an eye, a tooth for a tooth. Brazil, for example, has institutionalized *reciprocidade* as the linchpin to its foreign policy and will bitterly recall the austerity measures of the 1980s advocated by the US. But such a response violates the golden rule of "do[ing] unto others as you would have them do upon you."[38] There are plenty of poor people throughout the North who do not own any home, much less second and third homes, who do not have any car, much less a Hummer, and so on. They did not overshoot the CO_2e. They too are victims. *La crisis, ¡que la paguen los ricos!* must refer to the rich in the rich countries. Again, such accountability is fairly obvious and obviously fair.

In "The Tragedy," Hardin wrote "After reaching what seems to be an unavoidable conclusion, one must endeavor to shuck off one's commitment and examine the conclusion as an unfriendly opponent would. Changing places, can one see another possibility?"[39] When it comes to taxes, misery loves company. The rich in the rich countries will turn my fairness argument on its head. Why should the rich in the poor countries be exempt? They have a point and their fellow rich in the poor countries have also overshot CO_2e and should not be exempt. The tax on the rich should be global with the same wealth threshold irrespective of national origin. Such a proposal integrates with those of Susan George concerning global taxes for environmental ends and would prevent tax-driven international migration.[40]

All of this may sound contradictory to the *realpolitik* invoked in explaining resource allocation. Won't extremely wealthy people resist any new tax tooth and nail? They will resist and their anticipated resistance is why the type of tax must be chosen strategically. New taxes on income or assets will meet the strongest resistance and should be avoided. Inheritance tax will meet the least resistance for the simple reason that the rich person is dead when the taxman cometh. How much should be levied is a function of how much will be needed to get the carbon-rich Southern countries through the bottleneck from the cowboy economy to that of a spaceship. My gut feeling is that the number will be extremely high given the large populations in many of the carbon-rich countries (e.g. China and India). That feeling is at variance with the rosy picture of win-win situations painted by Jeffrey Sachs and others.[41] The economics of the Yasuní-ITT Initiative implies that the UNDP Human Development Index must rise substantially for countries of hundreds of millions of people (e.g. Indonesia and Nigeria) and a billion plus people (China and India) without the CO_2e emissions that have historically accompanied economic development. The challenge will not be cheap or easy. Ecuador can serve as a test case.

With the overview of a global inheritance tax established, we must now delve into the details. I will start with a simple assumption (once an economist always an economist): people naturally want to see their descendants live a materially comfortable life. Such a life can be considered the one enjoyed by the 95th percentile in the industrialized North. For example, the lower limit of the 95th percentile of income in the US was $166,000 in 2005.[42] Assuming a very conservative return on investment of 2%, the wealthy can guarantee that their descendents will enjoy the 95th percentile of income in perpetuity with a bequest of $8.3 million. In other words, all the assets of the rich over $8.3 million per child (or two named beneficiaries should the rich be childless) should be collected in an inheritance tax. This means that the estate of a billionaire with three children, would pay all but $24.9 million to the State. Is that unreasonable?

Unexpected supporters of this proposal may be some of the billionaires. They also intuit the impact of their over-consumption on the planet just as many intuit that birth into extreme luxury has undermined the values of their children. If they wish to secure a comfortable life in perpetuity for their bloodline, that line can live off the annuity. If at any moment a generation in that line wishes to be a biological dead-end, it can consume the capital of $8.3 million. Once all carbon-rich countries have reached the threshold in the Human Development Index that Costa Rica reached in 2001 when it declined to extract its petroleum, the global inheritance tax can expire.

Combining the nature of *realpolitik* with that of NET, one notes that the extremely rich are also bifurcation points whose interests are amplified through highly paid lobbying. No doubt there will be belligerent points triggered by my proposal. Nowhere will that belligerence be more vehement than in the US where, in 2009, a bipartisan bill was introduced in the Congress to lower the top tax rate on inheritances from 45% to 35%. It would affect 0.2% of estates and was introduced amidst two ongoing wars, a great recession, a health care crisis, and a projected budget deficit exceeding a trillion dollars. Should the bill somehow succeed, $250 billion in revenues will be foregone over ten years.[43] By implication, my proposed inheritance tax would generate approximately $1.375 trillion from the US alone over the ten year period, roughly $128 billion per year or 100 times that needed in any given year to initiate the Yasuní-ITT Initiative.[44]

Honoré de Balzac maintained that "behind every great fortune there is a crime."[45] The accuracy of "every" is debatable (most? many? some? a few?) but less debatable is the update "behind every great fortune there is a gush of CO_2e." The super-rich who made their fortune by hook or by crook often find bequeathing a dilemma. One thinks of the American ex-convict Leona Helmsley and her Maltese lap dog "Trouble." As reported upon her death, Ms. Helmsley was "[t]he woman who famously said 'only the little people pay taxes,' [and] decided that a little dog gets the largest single bequest from her inheritance. Just to recap, Leona Helmsley died last week leaving a $4 billion fortune made by investing in luxury hotels, cheating on taxes and abusing employees."[46] By the economics of the Yasuní-ITT Initiative, the Leona Helmsleys of the world will still be able to spend their fortunes on goods and services, subject to carbon taxes and cap-and-trade, and leave multiple millions (but not billions) to their descendants or their dogs.

The paragraph above began with a reference from a giant in French Letters. This paragraph and this chapter will end with a reference from another literary genius, the German Thomas Mann. Like the family Buddenbrooks,[47] I suspect that four generations onward, many descendants of the super-rich will have completely de-capitalized no matter how great the fortune left by the original entrepreneur. Realizing this, the multi-millionaires, the billionaires, and the multi-billionaires of today can create a legacy that is truly sustainable – a green capitalization in the carbon-rich countries – and help take their descendants and the planet through the treacherous bottleneck from the cowboy to the spaceship economy.

Chapter 4

THE GENERAL THEORY OF SECOND BEST

A Rigorous Justification for an Intuitively Just Proposal

Robert W. Fogel won the 1993 Nobel Memorial Prize in Economics "for having renewed research in economic history by applying economic theory and quantitative methods in order to explain economic and institutional change."[1] Clio was the muse of history and Fogel applied the new "cliometrics" to accounting records of slave transactions. In 1974, he and Stanley Engerman published *Time on the Cross: The Economics of the American Negro Slavery*. The analysis refuted the popular narrative that ran something like this

- The slave system was economically moribund;
- Union soldiers, fired up by abolitionist presses, died in vain;
- Slaves would have soon been freed anyway;
- The rising tide of sentiment pro-abolition in the North had little to do with secession of the Confederate States in the South.[2]

Although exposing mythologies is healthy for any democracy, such analysis can also be misconstrued. For example, Fogel and Engerman note that "...the evidence that is beginning to accumulate suggests that the attack on the material conditions of the life of blacks after the Civil War was not only more ferocious, but in certain respect, more cruel than that which preceded it."[3] Was slave-life better than freedom? The question is loaded and invites an affirmative response which is both facile and repugnant. A holistic response is the stuff of the general theory of second best. "The attack on the material conditions of life after the Civil War" means that the government failed to intervene in a way that would put the freed slaves on a path of material well-being.

Through the lens of second best, slavery is an intricately distorted system whose nature undermines the bedrock assumption of all economic theory: self-interest. Absence of self-interest constitutes the supreme distortion of the market economy and makes mockery of "It is not from the benevolence of the butcher, the brewer, or the baker, that we expect our dinner, but from their regard to their own interest."[4] To induce self interest, the slaveholder would use not just the stick (the driver) but also the carrot (the institution of "manumission"). Slaves would receive bonuses for performance and, in their declining years, could spend those savings in buying their own freedom. In Spanish, we call this a "negocio redondo" – a business that cannot lose! However, as Fogel and Engerman point out, manumission sets up a contradiction: if the slaveholder "owns"[5] the slave and the slave owns a dollar, then by transitivity the slaveholder also owns that dollar. Through the lens of second best, manumission is a necessary distortion to make the slave system efficient, given the distortion of no self-interest on the part of the slaves.

Second best also sheds light on the post-Civil War period. The historic epoch of Reconstruction had to contend with the removal of the supreme distortion to a market economy (the lack of self-interest) as well as the emergence of new distortions among the now free agents (dependency and distrust from centuries of oppression). In light of these new distortions, second best implies that adding still more distortions would have made the post-Civil War economy more efficient. Among the needed distortions for a successful Reconstruction would have been free adult education for the illiterate masses and land distribution for landless masses.[6]

Had the US government so distorted the market system, emancipation would probably have avoided the ferocious and cruel "attack on the material conditions of the life of blacks" so well documented by Fogel and Engerman.

Did large-scale intervention occur to anyone at the time? Following the infamous March to the Sea (1865), Major General William Tecumseh Sherman issued Special Field Orders No. 15 to confiscate 400,000 acres from slave plantations along the Atlantic Coast of South Carolina, Georgia, and Florida and distribute the lands in 40 acre parcels to the 100,000 freed slaves, along with surplus army mules. The "40 acres and a mule" is often considered "compensation," albeit nominal, for the horrors that African Americans endured during slavery.[7] Again the choice of language channels the debate. Whatever the intentions of Sherman, be they noble (compensation to the victims) or ignoble (retribution against the vanquished), the equity of the Special Field Orders No. 15 can be analyzed in terms of efficiency. Had the former slaves become homesteaders, American history would have been infinitely better. One can easily imagine the robust economy of a hundred thousand family farms along the Atlantic Coast instead of the rural poverty that persists to this day. Unfortunately, racism triumphed in post-Civil War America.[8] President Andrew Johnson reversed Special Order No. 15 in 1868 and so began a century of *de facto* slavery through segregation and disenfranchisement. Three generations after the Civil War, William Faulkner, the 1949 Nobel Laureate of Literature from Mississippi would write "[t]he past is never dead[,] [i]t's not even past."[9] Analysis of the economic impact of American racism and the vicious cycles of poverty would earn Gunnar Myrdal the 1974 Nobel Memorial Prize in Economics.

History invites analogies. With respect to climate fluctuations and the Yasuní-ITT Initiative, we are in a "40 acres and a mule" moment. My analogy with American slavery is almost complete and lacks only a few details. Primary among them is that the vast majority of the citizens of the Confederacy States of America owned no slaves. The slave-owning aristocracy conscripted poor white men, eighteen percent of whom would die.[10] It was cost-shifting success writ large. As we see from US history, efficiency and equity are not separate issues. Given the non-negotiable value judgment of freedom, what would have been equitable (40 acres and a mule) would have also been efficient. Now for the analogy: given the non-negotiable value judgment of no cost-shifting for anthropogenic climate fluctuations, the industrialized North should pay the carbon-rich South to keep the carbon underground and earmark the funds for the transition to a sustainable development.

One may agree with the idea of compensation but disagree that it should begin with the ITT oil fields of Yasuní, which is but a drop in the bucket for future CO_2 emissions. James Hansen, arguably the world's leading climatologist and head of the NASA Goddard Institute for Space Studies, puts it this way, "Coal is responsible for as much atmospheric carbon dioxide as all other fossil fuels combined and is even more of a long-term threat given the earth's enormous coal reserves."[11] With vast coal reserves, priority for compensation should go to China and India. So, why are we discussing the economics of the Yasuní-ITT Initiative and not a China-India coal initiative? The answer is efficiency. Like any engineering proposal, a pilot project is prudent before embarking on any large scale investment. From a global perspective, Ecuador can serve as the pilot for figuring out how implementation would work before scaling up to Indonesia, Nigeria, India and China. To make my analogy complete with American slavery, Ecuador-as-pilot-project would be like the United States having experimented with "40 acres and a mule" first in tiny Delaware, before tackling the plantations of the Atlantic Coast of South Carolina, Georgia, and Florida.[12]

A large segment of the public finds historical analogies unpersuasive. They feel "the fierce urgency of now." So more examples are needed. Let me offer one that is *au courant*. I will apply the theory of second best to current events from my corner of the world (Puerto Rico). As I write, (May 2009) the Puerto Rican economy is in the worst recession since the Great Depression. Economists do not agree on the definition of depression and three consecutive years of negative growth may even qualify the downturn as a depression. Be that as it may, the theory of second best manifests itself with a vengeance. Governor Luis Fortuño began his term on January 1, 2009 on a neoliberal platform. In the midst of declining tax revenues, a monstrous debt, and dreams of US statehood, Fortuño introduced Law No. 7 to encourage some 30,000 people off the public payroll through "renuncias voluntarias [voluntary resignations]."[13] The goal would be reduction of roughly 10% of government workers. As of May 2, 2009, less than 1% responded (only 2,495 people) and many were the underpaid public school teachers who are difficult to retain much less recruit. The unintended consequence of Law No. 7 was foreseeable from the theory of second best. Addressing the distortion of tenured public service jobs through incentives to resign aggravated the distortion that teachers are not paid market salaries. Familiarity with second best should give pause to any politician bent on piecemeal reform.

An indicator of the usefulness of any economic theory is its applicability across the political spectrum. The theory of second best easily meets that criterion. Both critics and advocates of neoliberal reform can construct second best arguments to make their points even regarding the same market! Examples that have nothing to do with oil illustrate the robustness of second best thereby strengthening the case for its application to oil.

Let us further develop the example from the academic labor market, my personal favorite. Neoliberals the world over are opposed to institution of tenure ostensibly because it undermines the accountability of faculty and induces "moral hazard," i.e. shirking once one has the guarantee of lifetime employment. Faculties the world over rejoin that tenure protects research into areas that go against the corporate interests that co-opt governments. One thinks of Big Oil, Biotech, Wall Street, and the professors who have studied climate fluctuations, genetically modified organisms, and the backdating of stock options. Could they have done so without tenure? Perhaps they could have. Would they have done so? Many would not have assumed the risks of job dismissal. Although academic freedom justifies tenure, one must recognize tenure as a distortion to the academic labor market. By the wisdom expressed by the co-discover of second-best, Richard Lipsey, and quoted at length in Chapter 2, "any policy may have unexcpected and undesirable consequences in apparently unrelated parts of the economy that need to be watched for and mitigated."[14]

No awareness of the theory of second best was evident in January 1994 when the Age Discrimination in Employment Act of 1967 (ADEA) was extended to cover tenured faculty members facing mandatory retirement ages.[15] The removal of the distortion *seemed* to enhance efficiency. Mandatory retirement is inefficient if a 70 year old wants to work and performs with excellence. However, in the light of second best, the removal of one distortion (mandatory retirement) may exaggerate another (tenure) and make the system less efficient (an underperforming and aged faculty). Not just septuagenarians but also octogenarians and even nonagenarians can hang on to their university jobs. If the one removes one distortion (mandatory retirement at 70), then one must remove the related distortion (tenure beyond 70). In other words, if one accepts the notion of tenure (for very good reasons) then one must also accept the idea of compulsory retirement (due to second best) at some age.[16]

The examples of second best from education illustrate the political neutrality of the theory. I repeat: just as it can be used to critique neoliberal reform, it can also be used to defend it. Everything depends on context which coheres with the overarching theme of the theory of second best: economies are complex systems that suffer multiple distortions. Nevertheless, the examples may seem to veer from the question at hand: the economics of climate fluctuations and the case whether or not Ecuador should be paid for not extracting the petroleum from the ITT oilfields. So let me turn to a more relevant example of applying second best thinking: the Organisation of Petroleum Exporting Countries (OPEC). Had Venezuela not spearheaded the cartelization of oil in the early 1960s, the world would have suffered greater CO_2 emissions and a more precipitous onset of climate transformation. Cartelization permitted OPEC to reduce the supply of petroleum as it sought the profit-maximizing level of world production. Predictably, textbooks of introductory economics cite OPEC only negatively.[17] Students are taught that oligopolies not only cause a "deadweight loss" to consumers who could have enjoyed the cheap oil, but also inefficiencies in production, as the quantity supplied is not at the lowest point of costs on the average cost curve. Suppressed in such presentations is the persistent externality of CO_2 emissions and the continued success of industry in shifting those costs. The omission coheres with the flawed concept of the circular flow of the economy between households and firms as discussed in Chapter 1. Although dampening CO_2 emissions was an unintended consequence of OPEC, the world should nevertheless be grateful. In the abstract terms of second best, the OPEC cartel is a distortion as are the unaccounted CO_2 emissions. The addition of select distortions (cartelization) to an already distorted economy (cost-shifting) improved the efficiency of the system (fewer climate fluctuations).

At a "macro" level among countries, second best applies to the Yasuní-ITT Initiative for the reasons cited in the first chapter: the absence of a cap is a distortion which requires the distortion of compensation to make the system more efficient, viz., manageable levels of CO_2e emissions. No doubt the critics of the Yasuní-ITT Initiative will get self-righteous. After all, they will argue, the newly industrializing carbon-rich countries are committing the same cost-shifting success of which they accuse the industrialized North. The trouble with such an argument is that it ignores the *realpolitik* of those newly industrializing countries where the choice for politicians is between improving the welfare of its impoverished citizens or protecting the welfare of people beyond its borders (one thinks of low-lying Bangladesh). The certifiable genius Freeman Dyson notes, "There's a lot of truth to the statement Greens are people who never had to worry about their grocery bills...the move of the populations of China and India from poverty to middle-class prosperity should be the great historic achievement of the century. Without coal it cannot happen."[18] Dyson's sentiment recalls Hardin's quote that *"the morality of an act is a function of the state of the system at the time it is performed."*[19]

If the general theory of second best is indeed robust, it should apply not only to Ecuador within the community of nations, but also to the communities within the nation of Ecuador. Specifically, second best can apply to national policy regarding land use and climate transformation.

Let me give one last example that could not be more custom-made to the issues of global climate stabilization. Shortly after the signing of the Kyoto Protocol in 1997, I had the good fortune to be the director of an excellent Master's thesis from the Facultad Latinoamericana de Ciencias Sociales (FLACSO). It was about the theory of second best, the Clean Development Mechanism of the UNFCCC and agricultural land use. The student, Aida Arteaga, examined three farms in Ecuador.[20] Two were adjoining farms in a mountainous region and both raised cattle. The first (whimsically named Bombolí) preserved all the forest cover on the hillsides, roughly 30% of the land. The neighboring farm preserved only 7% of the forest cover. The third farm was the experimental station (Centro Fátima) in a high altitude region of the Amazon (900m) and raised native animals which grazed on a natural succession of forest growth. The estimates of CO_2e emissions were surprising. Bombolí had much more water than did the neighboring farm and water was the limiting factor in cattle-raising. When one computed the CO_2e of the flatulence (CH_4) of the additional cattle, Bombolí with its 30% forest cover had a worse carbon impact than the farm with only 7% forest cover! In other words, reforesting the hillsides of degraded pasture would be counterproductive for the purpose of reducing net greenhouse gas emissions. The absence of cattle in the baseline of greenhouse gas emissions is a distortion that would be amplified by reforestation.

Greater CO_2e through reforestation is one of the many unintended consequences of piecemeal policy reform that is explicable and predictable from the theory of second best. But second best can also suggest policies. Reforestation is an increase in the carbon pool only if one raises the native sources of animal protein as in the case of Centro Fátima. Given the causation of CO_2e emissions lies in the manufacture of dietary preferences (e.g. the media campaigns for Big Mac's, Whoppers, and Burrito Supremes), second best suggests a countervailing governmental intervention into the formation of preferences for the protein sources that are natural to the habitat of secondary growth forests.

Although my argument tries to appeal to a wide readership through varied examples of second best, ranging from the horrors of American slavery to the whimsically named Bombolí, it is nevertheless encumbered by abstractions peculiar to my profession. Why do I and other economists talk about second best when "unintended consequences" would be more easily understood? Translating my examples into plain English, one could say that the unintended consequence of:

- emancipation was deteriorated material well-being of the freedmen
- incentives schemes for resignation of public employees motivated resignation of only those employees who were of greatest value
- dismantling mandatory retirement allows "working" until one dies of old age
- reforestation of pastures generates greater greenhouse gas emissions.

Fogel and Engerman recognize the complaint about choice of language in *Time on the Cross*:

To many humanists, the work of the 'softer' social scientists frequently appears pretentious. Very often one has to work extremely hard to decipher the jargon of a social scientist, only to discover a generalization about human behavior previously noted by Shakespeare, with fewer footnotes but with much greater wit and elegance.[21]

"Unintended consequences" is indeed a favorite theme of Shakespeare and so, the humanist may press on. Why not a citation of Hamlet's erroneous slaying of Polonius and its train of disastrous events? Fogel and Engerman provide an answer that would resonate throughout scientific audiences no matter what the discipline. "Arguments that rest on impressionistic fragmentary evidence must be considered to be on a relatively low level of reliability, regardless of the objectivity of the source of the evidence."[22] For problems that lend themselves to a technical solution, Fogel and Engerman are 100% correct. One must dismiss anecdotes as committing the statistical error of small sample size and metaphors as rhetorical flourishes without much merit.[23] But they are wrong, albeit not 100% wrong, for problems that do not lend themselves to a technical solution. As argued from the first chapter onward, climate fluctuations and transformation belong to the class of problems that has no technical solution.

Hardin's solution to the class of problems that has no technical solution is "mutual coercion, mutually agreed upon." The language of any economic proposal must be inviting for discussion rather than intimidating. Scientific rigor forms a filter against the participation of most people who have not assimilated the scientific method. For that reason, Fogel and Engerman are not 100% wrong in their insistence on rigor – eggheads are indeed present – but they may be closer to 100% than most professors of economics would like to think. Edward E. Leamer, an econometrician at the University of California at Los Angeles, tells a reporter to *The Chronicle of Higher Education*:

> the era of Samuelson…was so successful in introducing mathematics into the conversation that it's now required that you speak math…because most of our PhD students can never really master that language, and they struggle so hard with the grammar and syntax that they end up not being able to say anything… A mathematician is uninterested in the problem…He's interested in the degree of difficulty of the proof, or the surprise nature of the theorem. Those value systems are fine in mathematics, but they're very destructive in economics.[24]

If PhD students in economics struggle with the language of math, then one can only imagine the frustration of the general public. Even the relatively straightforward concept of "market failure" will tax its patience.[25] Totally inappropriate are arguments couched in a math that would give pause even to the PhD student of economics (e.g. the isoelastic function for utility or the balanced growth equivalent of the discounted computation path, found in *The Stern Review*) .[26]

In an anthology of the best popular writing in science and nature, E. O. Wilson perceives a barrier seldom discussed in the climate debate:

> To enjoy [the scientific method] while maintaining an effective critical attitude requires mental discipline. The reason, again, is the innate constraints on the human brain. Gossip and music flow easily through the human mind, because the brain is genetically predisposed to receive them....Trust me: physics is hard even for physicists.[27]

Like physics, economics is hard even for economists. Arguments which teeter on a scaffolding of assumptions and expressed in complex equations are simply not understood. If not being understood is indeed intentional, then we have "the Argument from Blinding with Science (in this case mathematics)."[28] Nevertheless, understanding mathematical concepts like statistical significance and exponential growth are necessary for living within limits based on "mutual coercion, mutually agreed upon." Fortunately, one does not need a scientific education to become conversant in the discussion. I would even hazard the hypothesis that pre-literate people understand statistical significance and exponential growth better than a significant number of college graduates who have been formally exposed to both.

I have peppered this and previous chapters with refrains, some of which border on clichés. An appropriate one here would be "One swallow does not make a spring." It captures the mathematical concept of small sampling size bias while exploiting the biophilia (love of life) of our adapted minds. Similarly, the concept of exponential growth is seen in metaphors that tellingly reflect biophobia (fear of life): to spread like wildfire, like a weed or like the plague. College graduates often lack first-hand experience with conflagrations, gardening, and epidemics and therefore have a more difficult time assimilating "mutual coercion, mutually agreed upon" than would their pre-literate or marginally literate farming ancestors. Indeed, the adapted mind does not assimilate the purely cognitive experiences of school, and educators have long recognized as much. Benjamin S. Bloom was the first to formalize the distinct domains of learning.[29] Within the cognitive domain, the challenge is to climb the pyramid of learning from lowest level of acquiring knowledge to the highest of evaluating theoretical frameworks while incorporating the affective and psycho-motor domains.[30]

The adapted mind is finely tuned to detect deception and "cost-shifting success" is deception *par excellence*.[31] Whereas people will tune out when they hear "market failure" and turn off with isoelastic utility functions or the discounted computation path, neurons will fire with "cost-shifting success." Hardin intuited that the adapted mind is part of the solution toward "mutual coercion, mutually agreed upon." As a cognate to "literacy," and "numeracy," he coined the word "ecolacy" and observed that:

> No doubt words were used before numbers; but in a primitive way, the ecolate view may be older than either of the two. What sophisticated people interpret as unintelligent conservatism on the part of 'primitive' people generally springs from an 'instinctive' nonverbal recognition of the complexity of life.[32]

Because climate transformation is a problem without a technical solution, the challenge is to engage people to perceive the necessity of living within limits. However, reliance on the authority of the experts raises suspicions. Not even experts in one field will automatically defer to experts in another. One sees this in Dyson's dismissal of Hansen,

> If what he says were obviously wrong, he wouldn't have achieved what he has. But Hansen has turned his science into ideology. He's a very persuasive fellow and has the air of knowing everything. He has all the credentials. I have none. I don't have a Ph.D. He's published hundreds of papers on climate. I haven't. By the public standard he's qualified to talk and I'm not. But I do because I think I'm right. I think I have a broad view of the subject, which Hansen does not. I think it's true my career doesn't depend on it, whereas his does. I never claim to be an expert on climate. I think it's more a matter of judgment than knowledge.[33]

Through discussion between climate experts and the public, many of the skeptics will become receptive to "mutual coercion, mutually agreed upon." Dyson himself is a good candidate inasmuch as his major concern is that an unfair deal is in the works which would cap greenhouse gas emissions and effectively lock poor carbon rich countries out of development. The Yasuní-ITT Initiative would allay that concern.

The French philosopher Jacques Ellul remarked:

> Democracy is based on the concept that man is rational and capable of seeing clearly what is in his own interest, but the study of public opinion suggests this is a highly doubtful proposition…Public opinion is so variable and fluctuating that government could never base a course of action on it; no sooner would government begin to pursue certain aims favored in an opinion poll, than opinion would turn against it…Only one solution is possible: as the government cannot follow opinion, opinion must follow the government. One must convince this present, ponderous, impassioned mass that the government's decisions are legitimate and good and that its foreign policy is correct.[34]

In sum, the general theory of second best is a rigorous justification for an intuitively just proposal – the Yasuní-ITT Initiative. The public must be sufficiently engaged to support governments who assume leadership in implementing it. That leadership must begin simultaneously in the North and South. Am I hopeful?

Chapter 5

THROUGH THE BOTTLENECK OF A COWBOY ECONOMY

Financing Shovel-Ready Projects

Theory does not happen in a vacuum. Economists will think of John Maynard Keynes and the Great Depression.[1] Keynes observed that markets do not always clear as economics had long taught. For example, one third of US labor force was effectively without work in the 1930s.[2] Rather than prices, quantities adjusted and the economy settled into an unemployment equilibrium. By incorporating that observation into theory, macroeconomics emerged.[3] Today, more reason exists than ever to believe that theory cannot happen in a vacuum. According to Stern, climate fluctuations may wreak havoc on the scale of the Great Depression and the wars of the first half of the twentieth century combined.[4] Will a new macro-macroeconomics emerge? The crux of my argument is that it has already emerged. By the mid-1970s, a new macro-macroeconomics could be gleaned in the economics of Boulding, Georegescu-Roegen, Schumacher, and Daly, and the science of Carson, Ehrlich, Hardin, and Prigogine. Ten years is a reasonable lag for putting into practice the synthesis. Had the political establishment acted by the mid-1980s, Stern's example of "climate change" as "market failure… on the greatest scale the world has seen"[5] would have been largely mitigated or even averted.

Incorporation of the second law of thermodynamics into economics is the necessary condition to address climate fluctuations but it is not sufficient. One must also understand how institutions work and collective decisions are taken. In the language of thermodynamics, institutions define the boundary conditions while the decisions taken become points of bifurcation in pathways of success or failure. With respect to the emergent pathways in CO_2e emissions, the Secretariat to the UNFCCC vets proposals through the Conference of the Parties (COP). Although none has advanced sufficiently to be labeled a success, it is still early in historical terms. What is not in dispute is how to get through the bottleneck of an underdeveloped carbon economy to a developed carbon economy.[6] Dirty industrialization is the tried-and-true recipe. A promising pathway to success in sustainability is a heavy Northern investment in the economically poor but carbon-rich countries so that they too can assume the caps of a global cap-and-trade system. Indeed, until they pass through the bottleneck, *realpolitik* militates against adoption of any cap. Ecuador hopes to become the model with the Yasuní-ITT Initiative.

The argument is simple and simplicity is an advantage in explaining the theory to the public. However, simplicity is also a disadvantage in putting that theory into practice. The devil is in the details. Fortunately, Hardin has provided not just a theoretical skeleton for management of the atmosphere but also many of the details. I have cited him frequently and to deploy a metaphor appropriate for the cowboy economists who may be reading, I believe that there is much more gold in "dem dere mountains."

Amazingly, Stern cites Hardin just once in *The Stern Review*: a textbox entitled "Tragedy of the Commons?" As presaged by the question mark, Stern bemoans Hardin's "commons" as an "oversimplified metaphor."[7] *No lo contendere.* The "commons" substitutes for "open access" which is the more accurate but less engaging expression. However, Hardin's equivocation on the word "commons" is probably not the reason why Stern and other academics do not give Hardin his due.[8] A better explanation is the hard edge in Hardin's prose. Consider, for example, Hardin's 1974 essay "Lifeboat Ethics: The Case Against Helping the Poor."[9] Stephen A. Marglin is typical of economists sympathetic to the ecological approach but no fan of Hardin. In the context of climate fluctuations, Marglin writes of Hardin "focusing blame on the poor seems misplaced. The major contributors both to environmental degradation and to resource depletion are the rich countries, not the poor countries."[10] One can easily imagine what would have been Hardin's response and then explore its relevance to Yasuní-ITT Initiative. To get to the gold of Hardin, we need look no further than the first page of "Lifeboat Ethics" and start analogizing:

> I can hear US liberals asking 'How can you justify slamming the door once you're inside? You say that immigrations should be kept out. But aren't we all immigrants, or the descendants of immigrants? If we insist on staying must we not admit all others?' [11]

Swapping words, we have:

> I can hear the critics of cap-and-trade asking 'How can you justify capping emissions once you've industrialized? You say that emerging economies should respect caps. But didn't we become developed because of a dirty industrialization? If we insist on imposing caps, must we not let them industrialize first?'

Hardin's rebuttal to the US liberal was

> …the logical consequence would be absurd. Suppose that, intoxicated with a sense of pure justice, we should decide to turn our land over to the Indians. Since our wealth has also been derived from the land, wouldn't we be morally obliged to give that back to the Indians too?[12]

The rebuttal I imagine Hardin would make to the critic of cap-and-trade emissions is

> …the logical consequence would be absurd. Suppose that, intoxicated with a sense of pure justice, we should let the tragedy of the commons ensue. Since our industrialization has also harmed their environments, wouldn't we be morally obliged to compensate for those damages too?

I am not setting up a straw man. The position of Bolivia in preparation for COPXV to the UNFCCC captures the logic of compensating the developing countries for the damages inflicted by the industrialization of the developed countries. According to the Bolivian position:

> The excessive past, current and proposed future emissions of developed countries are depriving and will further deprive developing countries of an equitable share of the much diminished environmental space they require for their development and to which they have a right. By over-consuming the Earth's limited capacity to absorb greenhouse gases, developed countries have run up an 'emissions debt' which must be repaid to developing countries by compensating them for lost environmental space, stabilizing temperature and by freeing up space for the growth required by developing countries in the future...
>
> Developing countries are not seeking economic handouts to solve a problem we did not cause. What we call for is full payment of the debt owed to us by developed countries for threatening the integrity of the Earth's climate system, for over-consuming a shared resource that belongs fairly and equally to all people, and for maintaining lifestyles that continue to threaten the lives and livelihoods of the poor majority of the planet's population. This debt must be repaid by freeing up environmental space for developing countries and particular the poorest communities.[13]

Like the position of "US liberals" on immigration, the Bolivian position on climate fluctuations will resonate with all people who cherish "pure justice." Always the wet blanket, Hardin provides an alternative to pure justice which will resonate with those who have the ultimate say, viz., the countries which end up paying. The last caption in "Life Boat Ethics" is "Pure Justice vs. Reality" and Hardin's thesis is sufficiently robust that no word substitutions are needed to appreciate its implications for the Yasuní-ITT Initiative:

> Clearly, the concept of pure justice produces an infinite regression to absurdity. Centuries ago, wise men invented statutes of limitations to justify the rejection of such pure justice, in the interest of preventing continual disorder. The law zealously defends property rights, but only relatively recent property rights. Drawing a line after an arbitrary time has elapsed may be unjust, but the alternatives are worse.[14]

Fortunately, for climate fluctuations, the line need not be drawn arbitrarily. It cannot be "1750"[15] as implied in the Bolivian position without "produc[ing] an infinite regression to absurdity." It can be drawn at 1990 when the IPCC recommended that emissions be cut by 60% to live within the threshold of a sustainable carbon cycle. Of all the details that will need to be fleshed out in the Yasuní-ITT

Initiative, a statue of limitations is the most critical. Only a handful of countries have come close to meeting the IPCC goal. The majority has increased their CO_2e emissions since 1990 and the variance among them implies that the payments should also vary.

Questions about other details easily flow. To whom should the compensation be directed? Thinking like Hardin-the-devil's-advocate is useful. If compensation were applied, as one may infer from the Bolivian position, "equally to all people" and "particular the poorest communities," then the system will be overwhelmed with claims and produce absurdity. It must be the poor countries among the group of carbon-rich countries.

A quick review of the questions and answers so far: when do claims begin? (answer: 1990); which countries should pay? (answer: those who surpassed the 60% reduction from the 1990 emission levels, in proportion to their excess emissions); and which should receive? (answer: the poor carbon-rich countries).[16] The final critical question of detail is this: "How long will the payments proceed?" If the answer is *ad infinitum*, then the North will anticipate donor-fatigue and obstruct. The Yasuní-ITT Initiative and similar endeavors cannot devolve into an industry of parties forever aggrieved.[17] So it is better to re-phrase the question. At what point in time should the developed countries no longer compensate the poor carbon-rich countries? As explained in Chapter 2, the world is fortunate for the example of Costa Rica. In 2001, Costa Rica refused to extract its offshore petroleum without any demand for compensation. When poor carbon-rich countries reach the threshold of the UN Human Development Index (HDI) of Costa Rica in 2001, payments can cease.

The Ecuadorian position to the UNFCCC can accommodate both the theoretical skeleton of "The Tragedy of the Commons" for management of the atmosphere as well as the details that arise from a close reading of Hardin's lifetime work. It also allows the horse-trading that must inevitably occur to get the country through the bottleneck of a cowboy economy:

Mitigation by Developing Countries
Nationally Appropriate Mitigation Actions (NAMAs) by developing countries
- In the framework of NAMAs, it is important to consider innovative options for developing countries, for example: to maintain petroleum underground (without exploiting) and to generate an economic

compensation in similar magnitude to that which the country would receive in case of exploitation, through mechanisms to be defined that will take advantage of past and present experiences.

Economic and social consequences of response measures

- Developing countries, whose economy essentially depends on fossil fuel exportation and production, are undergoing direct and indirect impacts by response measures of the developed world. These countries require a direct support to face the present and future.[18]

The four critical questions of detail could apply from the smallest to the largest economically-poor-but-carbon-rich country. In other words, the model is robust. Now comes the fifth critical question that must be specific to each poor carbon-rich country. How much direct support?

So far, I have been a bit evasive in providing sums about the transfer payments. Part of the reason, as explained in Chapter 1, is the volatile nature of the international petroleum and carbon markets. The other part is the asymmetry of negotiating power in international forums where tiny Ecuador is the David up against not just one Goliath but an army of Goliaths. The schema of Figure 5.1 is a simple heuristic for the estimate that awaits both refinement and negotiation. Roughly five billion dollars will be forgone in new infrastructure for petroleum extraction in the first four years after any international agreement of the Yasuní-ITT Initiative is reached. What interests vested interests in extracting the oil is, counterintuitively, not the oil that will flow but the investment stream. Elsewhere, I have called this SIMTO, solely-in-my-term-of-office.[19] Therefore, the schema must compete with other investment opportunities now.

A few statistics can anchor the calculations.[20] Approximately 850 million barrels lay below the ITT oils fields. The three fields could be exploited over a thirteen year time horizon. This translates to approximately 410 million tons of CO_2 avoided which generates anywhere from \$4 billion to \$12 billion depending on the carbon market (\$10 to \$30/ton, respectively). Without the Yasuní-ITT Initiative, the oil would have begun to flow in the fifth year meaning that compensation for the CO_2 avoided should also begin in the fifth year after consummation of any post-Kyoto agreement. For the sake of simplification of exposition, we can assume an even flow over that time horizon which means a yearly payment of approximately \$ 300 million to \$ 900 million per year for avoided CO_2 emissions. The transfer payment would stop immediately

Figure 5.1   Timeline of the Yasuní-ITT Initiative.

Year	0	1	2	3	4	5	Some Moment in the Future	Alternative Future Scenario
Event	Agreement					Post 2012 Agreement recognizes CO_2 avoided for carbon market	Ecuador achieves HDI of Costa Rica 2001 and assumes a cap	Ecuador auctions off ITT
Payment ($ millions)		1250	1250	1250	1250	300 to 900	0	Cessation of avoided CO_2 emission payments and exercise of claims against the Yasuní Guarantees plus compounded interests

when (1) Ecuador auctions off the ITT oilfields or (2) achieves the HDI of Costa Rica in 2001. Note well that the financial flows for carbon emissions avoided could extend beyond the thirteenth year if, God forbid, Ecuador has still not reached the level of HDI that Costa Rica reached in 2001. The reason is again *realpolitik*: the oil will still be underground and oh-so-tempting for future governments hell-bent on voiding the commitments of the Yasuní-ITT Initiative. In other words, payments cannot stop until a minimum threshold of development has been reached, perhaps earlier than year 13 or perhaps later. However, if some future Ecuadorian government decides on auctioning the ITT regardless of the HDI, payments would immediately cease and the government would be confronted with the clouding of claims on its exported oil by holders of the Yasuní Guarantees.

The nature of the money transferred warrants comment. We must not see the billions flowing over time as some species of foreign aid to Ecuador. If we do, the Initiative is a non-starter as the total foreign aid from all developed countries to all developing countries is only $120 billion.[21] The Initiative should be seen as an investment in a pilot project about how to stop long-run global climate transformation. To use the economic jargon favored by the UNFCCC, the transfer payment is "incremental" and does not substitute for any other foreign aid commitment to Ecuador or to any other country.

I have vetted the outline of the Initiative with economists knowledgeable about the issues. A typical response is that "it sounds a bit fishy."[22] The skepticism is understandable given that the economics of the Yasuní-ITT Initiative inheres in a thermodynamic approach which, albeit not new, is nevertheless revolutionary for policy-making (e.g. ideas such as bifurcation points, boundary conditions, and dissipative structures). In the thermodynamic approach, discounting future flows of benefits is rejected as it dooms the planet to climate transformation and mass extinction.[23] Similarly rejected is the argument that the oil stored will simply be replaced by other suppliers.[24] In the short-run it will, but violent climate fluctuations and mass extinction are all about the long-run. My critics may now cite Keynes and rejoin "in the long run we are all dead."[25] My reply is simple. Keynes was referring to individual humans and not the species *Homo sapiens sapiens*. At an instrumental level, the approach is also not subordinate to the criterion of "marginal abatement costs" which picks off the cheapest methods of carbon dioxide fixation worldwide, with no regard whatsoever to pathways of sustainable living traceable to bifurcation points and positive feedback mechanisms. The Yasuní-ITT Initiative is the product of thinking "outside the box." Again, one recalls the genius of Keynes who began *The General Theory* with:

> The ideas which are here expressed so laboriously are extremely simple and should be obvious. The difficulty lies, not in the new ideas, but in escaping from the old ones, which ramify, for those brought up as most of us have been, into every corner of our minds.[26]

To think outside the box, it also helps to live outside the box. In *An Inconvenient Truth*, Al Gore rakes Big Oil with a quote from Upton Sinclair "It is difficult to get a man to understand something when his salary depends upon his not understanding it."[27] Albeit true about Big Oil, it is no less true about environmental NGOs confronted with criticism from their moneyed opponents. For it not to be true about the Yasuní-ITT Initiative, the evaluation and selection of project proposals must be conducted by disinterested experts for whom no personal benefit depends upon which project is chosen. The need for such independence is consistent with mainstream economics. Alan S. Blinder makes the case for decisions by technocrats in his *Foreign Affairs* article "Is Government too Political?"[28] Judgment of proposals must be of the highest caliber as selection is a bifurcation point in the pathway through the bottleneck of a cowboy economy. A few general criteria should apply in the screening process. I list them below and follow each criterion with a brief explanation or example.

(1) *convincing public good aspects*
Many energy projects are appealing because they can yield a high commercial return. However, profitability undermines the case for government financing. Proposals must evidence an aspect of being a public good (non-rival in consumption and without any cost-effective mechanism of exclusion)

(2) *non-fungible with other public good projects*
Governments are already funding public goods to varying degrees. In the US, the Bill and Melinda Gates Foundation selected projects during the George W. Bush Administration I and II which were traditionally financed by the government.[29] In essence, their philanthropy freed public monies for war priorities. Proposals must possess some quality that previously frustrated government selection for funding.

(3) *platforms for different worlds which transcend the calculus of discounting future benefits*
Once we accept discounting streams of future benefits, we may as well close shop. Marglin puts it this way "at any rate around 5.75 percent, the *present value* of the benefits is less than the present value of the costs, even if the losses were ultimately 20 percent of global gross domestic product. In short, in terms of mainstream criteria, the case for incurring the costs of carbon stabilization is underwhelming. The only problem is that such analysis pretty much misses the point."[30] Proposals must afford a credible possibility of facilitating the emergence of a very different world, which does not collapse after a century-long consumption frenzy.

(4) *coherence with the overarching goal of stabilization of global CO_2 emissions and mitigation of the intertwined mass extinction crisis*
What economists cannot calculate in cost-benefit analysis, they tend to ignore which is equivalent to assigning it a value of zero. Such is the mainstream economic treatment of biodiversity. However, the alternative is not to invoke the caveat "this is best we can do" and calculate a number

which teeters on risible assumptions. Rather, one must create and evaluate cost-effective ways to live within limits. One of the most glaring deficiencies of *The Stern Review* is its blithe recognition but subsequent ignoring of the mass extinction crisis provoked by climate transformation. Proposals that somehow mitigate the extinction crisis must be candidates on equal footing with those that directly reduce CO_2 emissions.

(5) *beneficial impacts on traditionally disadvantaged groups*
In poor carbon-rich countries, such groups have multiple identities in a matrix of ethnicities, gender, sexualities, age, income, and geography. A new dimension emerges in the wake of climate fluctuations: the communities most threatened.

(6) *reflection of the preferences in the government of the collaborating countries from the North*
Money talks. *Realpolitik* means that the political leadership in the North will have to defend their decision to their own constituencies. Which proposals resonate among those audiences?

The criteria (1) through (6) reflect a way of thinking which accommodates many details but stops short of getting at the nitty-gritty. Because the details peculiar to each proposal will be beyond the expertise of the panel of judges, they too must avail themselves to experts within each specific field of the proposal. Fortunately, there is no shortage of experts of practical ideas. For example, the publishing house Earthscan boasts a title list about sustainability that reaches back twenty years. In the catalog for April 2009-September 2009, we have *Conservation and Biodiversity Banking: A Guide to Setting Up and Running Biodiversity Credit Trading Systems; Adapting Cities to Climate Change: Understanding and Addressing the Development Challenges; Planning for Climate Change: Strategies for Mitigation and Adaptation for Spatial Planners; Stand-Alone Solar Electric Systems: The Earthscan Expert Handbook on Planning, Design and Installation; Photovoltaics in the Urban Environment Lessons Learnt from Large Scale Projects;* and so on. All the cited books can be seen as springboards for international collaboration between Ecuadorian stakeholder institutions and international experts.

Nothing persuades like an example or two. Below are several that could help Ecuador pass through the bottleneck. Some challenge the fundamental assumptions of economics while others cohere completely with mainstream thinking. Inasmuch as non-fungibility is the second most important criterion in the half dozen listed above, it is worthwhile to identify which proposals challenge taboos inculcated in policymakers ever since their traumatic days in Economics 101.

Those that do should be chosen *ceteris paribus*. However, among the taboos, intensities will vary. Inspired by Hardin, the self-proclaimed "taboo-stalker," I will rank the intensity of taboo in the suggested proposals. When in conformity with economics, the proposal is represented by the naught symbol in the word "taboo", viz., tabøø (not a taboo). When at variance with the premises of mainstream thinking, the proposal is represented by repeated "o's" in the word "taboo," varying from the simple "taboo" to a real whopper, "taboooooooo." The latter requires greater explanation.

(1) *Lebensraum*:[31] Buffer zones along highways and agriculture-forest frontier through natural succession with subsequent harvesting of semi-domesticated native animals (taboo).

The managers would be paid for their custody of the area and could engage in sustainable agro-forestry activities.[32] Elsewhere, I have suggested "genesteading" where private holders of agroforestry parcels also engage in para-taxonomy and have a stake in any royalty stream from bioprospecting in the adjoining undisturbed forests. Although the potential of agriculture is recognized in *The Stern Review*, it is nevertheless hamstrung by mainstream thinking. Stern writes on reducing non-fossil fuel emission that "cuts will be more challenging to achieve in agriculture, the other main non-energy source."[33] The "challenge" is the taboo in economics of questioning the formation of preferences. Without a market for the food products of agro-forestry (e.g. tapir, capybara, snails), there is precious little incentive to do it. But preferences can be manufactured, as any parent knows whose child whines to visit Ronald McDonald® under the Golden Arches. It falls to government to promote new food preferences or resuscitate old ones that were once environmentally friendly.

Just as Ecuador should be paid for conserving its fuel underground, it should also be paid for avoiding emissions from reducing deforestation and forest degradation (the UN Collaborative Programme REDD). Again, Costa Rica provides a marvelous model. It protects approximately 25% of its natural habitat.[34] Until Ecuador achieves the HDI of Costa Rica in 2001, the government should be compensated for 25% protection of its habitat as a carbon credit through the post-Kyoto Protocol. In general, a premium should be paid for the differential percentage above the 25% standard. Countries with little forests should be paid an additional premium for reforestation until they reach 25% forest cover. Such incentives would avoid the perverse effects of second best, viz., deforesting to collect a carbon credit for subsequent reforestation or reforesting unsuitable habitats.[35] While the credits for the protected areas should remit to the government, the premiums for standing forests above 25% should remit to the private lands adjoining the protected areas - *lebensraum*. A schema for the aligning rewards is presented in the not-so-hypothetical example of five countries, labeled A through E in Figure 5.2 and 5.3. I leave it to the reader to identify the countries in Latin America. It is assumed that deforestation has occurred in three of the countries, no change in one of the countries, and reforestation in another from year 1 to year 2.

(2) A Pan-American Ciclovía (bike path) with three North-South axes, in the Amazon, in the Sierra, and in the Coast of Ecuador (taboo).

The bike paths that now weave through the capital city of Quito are hardly an alternative to city transport. They are narrow and cannot accommodate the necessary flows. One would need a bicycle highway with the width of

Figure 5.2 Aligning Incentives for Reducing Deforestation (Year One)

Country	A	B	C	D	E
Forest Cover Year 1	38%	3%	25%	25%	50%
Human Development Index (HDI)	Moderate	Low	Moderate	High	Moderate
Post-Kyoto Carbon Credits for % standing forest	25%	3%	25%	0%	25%
Differential which qualifies for a premium over carbon credit	13%	0%	0%	0%	25%
Differential which qualifies for a premium+ if reforested	0%	Up to 22%	0%	0%	0%

Figure 5.3 Aligning Incentives for Reducing Deforestation (Year Two)

Country	A	B	C	D	E
Forest Cover Year 2	36%	4%	24%	25%	49%
Human Development Index	Moderate	Low	Moderate	High	Moderate
Carbon Credit for % standing forest	25%	4%	24%	0%	25%
Differential which qualifies for a premium over carbon credit	11%	0%	0%	0%	24%
Differential which qualifies for a premium+ if reforested	0%	Up to 21%	1%	0%	0%

a normal two way auto road. This would be a major public works project that would absorb many un- and underemployed workers. Again, at play is the formation of preferences. One recalls that the Panamerican Highway was the result of a cultural hegemony which promoted car use from North to South America. A Panamerican Ciclovía, originating in Ecuador and looking both North and South, could challenge its neighbors to do likewise. The possible amplification effects are immense.[36]

(3) A chain of "Eco-Tambos" (lodges and restaurants) that become models for sustainable living. They could be spaced approximately 50 km apart which is one days' ride by bike on the Pan-American Ciclovía (taboo).

The lodges would be designed to maximize integration with the environments and also serve as demonstration models for a variety of sustainable technologies. Their construction would be metaphorical platforms for ecolacy using the techniques for adult literacy pioneered by the remarkable Paulo Freire.[37] One thinks of the well built and aesthetic lodges built in US National Parks by the WPA (Works Progress Administration) during the Great Depression. The Eco-Tambos should generate all their own energy needs and be aesthetically appealing to attract the tourist trade. Indeed, a chain of such lodges could even become a 21st century Santiago de Compostela eco-pilgrimage. The menu should be chosen for its environmental impact which means banning ecological insults like beef, mutton, tilapia and offering the tapir, capybara, and snails supplied from agroforestry projects. Above all, the lodges could also provide a service that defies the very language of mainstream economics: a vehicle for the emergence of community through local management.

(4) The institutionalization of a 'carbon offset tax' upon flight departure from Ecuador with the passenger opting for destination of the tax to a national or an international carbon dioxide fixation or biodiversity project. (tabøø).

Inasmuch as national projects would probably be more expensive than international opportunities (the unlikely scenario that Ecuador always remains the cheapest place to offset carbon or conserve biodiversity), the offset shows international cooperation as well as the effect of collaboration with Ecuador. The country of Bhutan has imposed rigor on its international tourists and with great success.[38] Why can't Ecuador? To be successful, the government would have to advertise the carbon offset tax as a signal of its commitment to worldwide sustainability. Because getting the price right is the mantra of mainstream economics, there is no taboo here.

(5) A national program that identifies demographic cohorts at risk of inopportune pregnancies and offers incentives to delay family formation (tabooooooo).

The idea was proposed by Garrett Hardin in *Living within Limits* and went nowhere. No doubt the sterilization campaigns in Puerto Rico in the 1950s and the forced abortions of China's one-child policy of the 1980s have stigmatized incentive mechanisms worldwide. However, one can promote population stabilization without promoting sterilization much less abortion. If adolescent girls were given a payment for not becoming pregnant (e.g. choosing abstinence), then the population may stabilize and even decline over time. The payments could be either in money or in kind.

The woman who illicitly ends a pregnancy to retain the flow of payments is probably even more receptive to not becoming pregnant in order to retain the flow of payments. If that plausible statement is true, the project will diminish clandestine abortions. It is an empirical question that can be tested. Nevertheless, anecdotes will exist where an abortion decision was motivated by the payments. Should the policy be to blame? Those who answer in the affirmative should contemplate an analogy in this era of global recession. Occasionally, a dismissed worker will reach for the gun and blow away the boss. US Postal Service workers call the phenomenon "going postal."[39] Is the contractual arrangement "employee-at-will" to blame? Should tenure be granted for every worker in every line of work? One does not need to invoke Hardin to realize how such tenure would "produc[e] an infinite regression to absurdity." If some countries heartlessly criminalize abortions, then the person who aborts is the alleged criminal, not the population policy. Nevertheless, I hasten to add that such criminalization is the epitome of misogyny and cruelty.

Tabooooooo morphs to tabøø, i.e., not a taboo for mainstream economics. With existing statistics from birth registries, one can map out the areas of the country and age cohorts according to probability of women experiencing an inopportune pregnancy. Women could voluntarily register at family planning clinics and receive a significant percentage of the monthly minimum wage salary, say 25%, for every month they are not pregnant until they reach an age, determined statistically, where the probability of an inopportune pregnancy declines. If money is too crass, then the compensation could be educational credits, with a greater redemption value reflecting the positive externalities of higher education. Through analysis of the probabilities, economists can figure out what is the optimal payment in each region to reduce inopportune pregnancy given the monies budgeted for the proposal. So, an integral part of the project is an interdisciplinary research unit composed of economists, statisticians, sociologists, anthropologists, and geographers.

The unintended consequence of the proposal is promotion of "traditional values." It is intentionally *pro* female, *pro* poor, *pro* countryside while also being, unintentionally, *pro* abstinence, *anti* abortion and *anti* divorce. The Catholic Church would be fool-hearty not to embrace it. However, by the very nature of taboos, such discussion may not even begin! Mainstream economists will also demur. The word "population" is not even indexed in *The Stern Review* and appears only indirectly in various models of climate change. In Section 9.5, Stern is loudly silent on the truth that reducing population will reduce the demand of carbon-intensive goods and services.[40] Surprisingly, natural scientists are also keeping company with the cowed social scientists. For example, the ecologist S. Pacala and the physicist R. Socolow published a highly visible paper in 2004 in *Science* entitled "Stabilization wedges: Solving the climate problem for the next fifty years with current technologies."[41] Absent was population as Paul and Anne Ehrlich quickly perceived, "Sadly, this otherwise fine paper neglected to mention obvious 'wedge' that could contribute – reduction in the population and growth rate and (ultimately) population size – and a less obvious one of encouraging a dietary shift away from beef and pork and toward poultry, fish, and vegetarian cuisine."[42]

The gold of Hardin glistens. In *Living within Limits: Ecology, Economics and Population Taboos*, Hardin opens with a vignette about Earth Day 1990 which marked the twentieth anniversary of the celebration and an increase in population of 47%. "When directors of philanthropic foundations and business concerns were solicited for financial support they let it be known that they would not look kindly on a population emphasis. Money talks, silence can be bought."[43] Fortunately, all is not despair when it comes to population policy. Some economists are breaking the tabooooo. For example, Sven Wunder, has created an ironic ten point formula for what governments can do to destroy forests with their new found oil wealth. The last point is "Abandon all family-planning programmes in favour of a pro-natalist strategy." Wunder writes "Point 10 on population policies is probably a controversial one, but is nevertheless included because it is a main underlying 'slow driver,' especially in respect of the expansion of land-extensive food crops."[44]

(6) A Museum of Bioprospecting, Intellectual Property, and the Public Domain (tabøø or taboo?).

The cartelization of genetic resources and associated knowledge will allow countries and communities to enjoy significant benefits from granting access to their genetic resources and associated knowledge.[45] Such limited monopoly rights are justified in mainstream economics due to the asymmetric costs of information creation, or in this case, conservation. So it is tabøø, viz., not a taboo. However, economists recoil at the justification of monopoly rents and so cartelization is, schizophrenically, also a taboo. To realize cartelization will requires massive infrastructure of databases at the community level.[46]

A museum would be an ideal venue to discuss cartelization as well as a host of emergent *sui generis* legislations regarding intellectual property and the protection of the public domain. For example, should geographic indications also extend to the signals of locations transmitted in commercial movies? Many movies filmed in Ecuador falsify the location as Colombia;

others invent a fictitious name for the country (e.g. *María Full of Grace* and *Proof of Life*). The damages from "geopiracy" await empiricism, but appear to run into the millions of dollars in forgone tourism.[47] Because the Museum clashes with moneyed interests, be they those of Big Pharma or of Hollywood, the proposal is more taboo than tabøø.

(7) A bureau which coordinates niche tourism and promotes service in sustainable projects (tabøø).

Market differentiation in "service tourism" has an illustrious trajectory in the US For example, the January/February 2009 issue of the magazine *SIERRA* lists 68 programs throughout the US where one actually pays a fee to work, exposing the canard of the work/leisure dichotomy in economic theory.[48] For example,

> Reclaiming the Rosillos, Big Bend National Park, Texas. February 28-March 7. Join us for our 16th year of service in Big Bend! We'll work on grasslands restoration and other projects to enhance the habitat and resources of this magnificent park. *Leader: James Moody. Price $495.*[49]

Such programs could be easily copied for work/leisure sojourns in Ecuador. The Yasuní National Park is one potential destination. The Travel Section of *The New York Times* featured the park in an article entitled "Feathers, Fur and Jungle Waters: In a vast Ecuadorean national park, a visitor treasures bird-watching and worries about oil-drilling."[50] On the front page was a photo captioned "squirrel monkey in Yasuní National Park in Ecuador, which is also a UNESCO preserve." The article included other pictures of the Quichua-run Napo Wildlife Center, Titi monkeys, cobalt-winged parakeets, a dugout canoe with a child, and an interior look at one of the well appointed bungalows. A bureau on niche service tourism could customize itineraries that include environmental collaboration, for everyone from the well heeled ("five days, four nights, $915 a person based on double occupancy"),[51] to the *mochileros* (backpackers) who may spend months in the country on less than twenty dollars a day. One notes that despite the recession which began in the US in 2007, US tourists to Ecuador soared in 2008 which is a hopeful sign indeed.[52]

(8) An Eco-Label-and-Link-Project (tabøø or taboo?).

The project would strive to eco-label all goods produced in Ecuador and upload the latest scientific evidence of environmental impacts on to the internet. Although "getting the price right" is the tiresome mantra of mainstream economics, externalities seldom get incorporated into the price of a good. As argued in Chapter 3, the internalization of externalities does not happen because market failure is actually cost-shifting success. As argued in criterion #4 above, many things defy monetization (loss of biodiversity) and hence the "right" price can never be found. Eco-labeling through eco-links enables disclosure and encourages scientific peer review. Once we know how we impact our environment through consumption choices, we can defy Hardin who pooh-poohed the appeal to conscience.[53] For example, in Latin America, there is a whole genre of adolescent experiments with Coca-Cola and Mentos.[54] An "Eco-Label-and-Link-Project" could be a Galbraithian countervailing power.

It would be erroneous to think the project is anti-business. On the contrary, eco-friendly factories and farms can promote their products through the links. For example, the shrimp exporter Expalsa has two videos which explain production methods and how its methods reduce CO_2 emissions.[55] Similarly, videos demonstrate "Fair Trade" in Ecuadorian coffee and bananas.[56] Through the project, experts can validate the claims.

(9) Collapse Tourism (Taboooooo).

Ecotourism almost always takes people to places that are still pristine. To the extent that the tour biases perceptions of the threatened ecosystems, such tourism causes harm.[57] Collapse tourism focuses on sites which are living within limits and those which have surpassed them. Its entertainment value lies not in the aesthetics of the place but in the intrigue of learning how to achieve "mutual coercion, mutually agreed upon." Through scientifically accurate portrayals, guides will reveal the scarred landscapes to the tourist. In Ecuador, tours could take tourists to the melting glaciers and the moraine, polluted rivers in the city and clean ones in the country, shrimp ponds and mangrove forests, soil erosion on cultivated 60 degree slopes and no-till farming, bleached and surviving reefs in the Galapagos, and so on.

Because "collapse tourism" hopes to morph political values for the imposition of limits, it becomes quintessentially taboooooo, second only to the population policy of proposal (5).

(10) Fugitive Emissions at PetroEcuador and elsewhere (tabøø).

Escape emissions account for a large share of CO_2 emissions worldwide. The famed inefficiencies of PetroEcuador are, if true, reason for hope. Fugitive emissions can be greatly reduced within the national network of extraction activities. The challenge is to spend the money allotted *for* fugitive emissions *on* fugitive emissions. Teams of international experts and auditors will be required.

(11) Faculty Awards at Regional Universities in Ecuador (tabøø).

Realpolitik is an integrating theme of my argument. Any portfolio of projects must include something for all major players, especially those who have the most to lose. Proposal number (10) may quell the protests within the powerful PetroEcuador. What will quell the protests that arise within the rich countries? One solution is to respect fully the intellectual property rights of the new technologies associated with all the proposals and favor adoption of those that use patented technologies from the collaborating countries. But that may not be enough. This last suggested proposal attempts to reach broadly across Ecuador and the collaborating countries.

A perennial problem in underdeveloped countries is migration from the countryside to the capital as rigorously studied by Sir Arthur Lewis, the 1979 Nobel Memorial Laureate in Economics. This is especially true for scholarly labor. The brain drain from the countryside to the capital continues from the capital to points overseas. A solution is to create a program that pays young academics a significant premium to locate at regional universities and launch projects in sustainable development. By the nature of being recently graduated, the inexperienced professor needs the *milieu* of an established institution. So, the project should also include a critical mass of seasoned foreign professionals for long term assignments at regional universities as well as a collaborative agreement with a foreign university for *practicums*.

Antecedents exist to promote scholarly exchange. In the US, the most notable is the Fulbright Program. Although the program has eroded since its inauguration in 1948, the erosion provides many useful lessons. Fulbright Awards are now for as little as two weeks and seldom granted for more than four months. Quantity has clearly adjusted but has quality? One suspects that it has also gone by the board. As of April 2009, the advertised scholarship for professors was approximately $2,800 per month when the average salary for an assistant professor ranges from $4,500 to $7,000 per month depending on field.[58] One doesn't have to be an economist to realize that accepting a Fulbright is a losing proposition, financially speaking. To work in sustainable development outside the capital city should not require a sacrifice from any professor, be he or she Ecuadorian or foreign. Not only must the salaries reflect a premium in the home country market, but the appointments should also be multi-year and not the laughable multi-week stints of the Fulbright awards. Evidence to the truth of that statement can be found in Ecuador. The stunning success of development in Salinas de Guaranda in the province of Bolívar has everything to do with a multi-decade commitment of the Salesian missionaries that began in 1971.

The monies generated from the Yasuní-ITT Initiative are significantly large to afford any and all of the eleven proposals suggested above and many more.

CONCLUSIONS

Reason for Hope and Despair

Politics is a reason for hope and despair. Al Gore is exemplary of how the politician can disabuse a public fervently engaged in denial. That alone is reason for hope. But Al's political career is *passé composé*. What about the leaders *du jour*? With science on the side of stabilizing atmospheric carbon, a new generation can impose the necessary limits. Voters in both the North and South have expressed a strong desire for "change we can believe in."[1] Is the supply of leaders meeting the demand? Unfortunately, in politics there is always reason for despair. Heads of state will find resilience in the system they campaigned to change; relentlessly, the system will try to change the politicians. The first sign of system resilience is a stream of incoherent messages as the politician transitions from the campaign trail to the seat of power. Pronouncements of fossil fuel exploration *and* a commitment to stabilizing atmospheric carbon is the doublethink that grips both the North and South.[2]

The saving grace is humor, the scarcest of all resources.[3] A clever turn of phrase can pierce the cold indifference of denial and expose the beguiling incoherencies. By the mid-1970s, the economist and polymath Nicholas Georgescu-Roegen had already surmised the fate of business-as-usual:

> Perhaps the destiny of man is to have a short but fiery, exciting, and extravagant life rather than a long, uneventful, and vegetative existence. Let other species – the amoebas, for example – which have no spiritual ambitions inherit an earth still bathed in plenty of sunshine.[4]

E. O. Wilson does not even give the amoebas a hail Mary pass. Black humor becomes green as Wilson contemplates the very worst:

> even if all life as we know it were somehow extinguished, these microscopic troglodytes [subsurface lithoauthotrophic microbial ecosystems] would carry on. Given enough time, a billion years perhaps, they would likely evolve new forms able to colonize the surface and resynthsize the precatastrophe world run by photosynthesis.[5]

Historians of science, take note. Darwin's famous closing to *The Origins of Species* would still be relevant, just without us "...from so simple a beginning endless forms most beautiful and most wonderful have been, and are being, evolved."[6] In Spanish, we call such reassurance *el consuelo de tontos* (the consolation of fools).

The possibility that catastrophic "climate change" will exterminate *Homo sapiens sapiens* is not contemplated in *The Stern Review*. Although the probability is low, it is not zero nor is it even news.[7] Carl Sagan entertained the possibility in his best-selling *Cosmos*, which was adapted into an immensely popular television series in 1980. The last episode, number thirteen, was entitled "Who Speaks for Earth?" Sagan remarked "[t]he runaway greenhouse effect on Venus is a valuable reminder that we must take the increasing greenhouse effect on Earth seriously."[8] Sagan further elaborated the point in 1994 in *Pale Blue Dot*:

> The climatological history of our planetary neighbor, an otherwise Earthlike planet on which the surface became hot enough to melt tin or lead, is worth considering – especially by those who say that the increasing greenhouse effect on Earth will be self-correcting, that we don't really have to worry about it, or (you can see this in the publications of some groups that call themselves conservative) that the greenhouse effect is a 'hoax.'[9]

Since 1994, the evidence from the European Space Agency about Venus shows just how prescient Sagan was.[10] The update from climate simulations on Earth is also ominous. The MIT Integrated Global Systems Model found the prospects of global warming twice as severe in 2009 as its previous estimates of 2003. Without massive action, the temperature will rise 5 degrees Celsius by the year 2100.[11] And beyond 2100? From the long sweep of human history, business-as-usual hazards group suicide and group suicide is indefensible.

Now a word *pro* suicide: for the individual and the couple, it can be both rational and ethical. One thinks of Garrett Hardin and his wife Jane who ended their long and devoted lives together, together. Hopeless suffering is absurd. Happily, the issue of choosing death is no longer taboo. Over the last ten years, a genre of life-affirming movies has emerged which extols not only suicide but also assisted suicide (e.g. *The Cider House Rules, Million Dollar Baby, The Sea Within*). Despite the merit in individual or double suicide, group suicide is never rational or ethical. One thinks of Jonestown, Guyana and the coercion to drink the Kool-Aid. With respect to a runaway greenhouse effect...can't we just wear pullovers in the winter? Hang up our clothes in the summer? Opt for having fewer children? Eat tofu?...Implement the Yasuní-ITT Initiative? My hope for humanity lies in the peculiar fact that hope defines humanity. At the level of the group, embracing limits for our long term survival coheres as much with our human nature as does the tragedy of the commons. Moreover, at the level of the individual, doing the right thing engenders a sense of purpose in a world seemingly devoid of meaning.

Hope is the bread and butter of Heads of States. Political handlers know that Cassandras never get elected to anything, much less to head a government. So, when the mandarins meet to define a course of action on a global problem, hope abounds. A skilful photographer can capture the mood on film. After you finish reading this sentence, please stop a moment and examine the official portrait of the G-20 Meeting held on April 2nd, 2009 in London (Figure C.1).

Sagan commented that a picture is worth not 1,000 words as the proverbial wisdom would have it, but the equivalent of 10,000 words or "bytes" of information.[12] Interpretation can compress all those unwieldy bytes into a coherent narrative. Looking at Figure C.1, one begins with color. From the electric sheen of the continents at dawn to the deep space both left and right, the color is in all shades of blue. Ever since the first photographs of Earth from the 1968 Apollo mission, blue has rivaled green for being environmental.[13] Most of

Figure C.1   "Family Photograph," The London Summit 2009.

Credit: Photo: Eric Feferberg/Agence France-Presse – Getty Images, 2009.
http://www.londonsummit.gov.uk/en/

the ties are also blue as is the lone turban.[14] From the position of the Earth in the logo, one deduces that the time is dawn on a summer day in the Northern hemisphere. Inasmuch as the cloud cover has been airbrushed away, the image implies that a meltdown is underway for the glaciers and permafrost of the Arctic. Tellingly, the world leaders have turned their back to the planet, which itself is eclipsed by the dominant ideology: STABILITY (illusory), GROWTH (more illusory), and JOBS (raw politics).[15] Could my interpretation be any more lugubrious?

What about the demeanor of the subjects? It is jovial! The proverbial man from Mars would never imagine that the agenda was a worldwide recession careening into a depression. Now let's do a thought experiment inspired by Photoshop®. Imagine cropping the leaders and flipping the group 180° on stage while keeping the backdrop stationary. In our minds, the leaders have now turned their back to us, their constituents. They are facing the banner THE LONDON SUMMIT 2009 and a few have their sight focused on

Figure C.2 Barack Obama, The London Summit 2009.

Credit: Lawrence Looi/Newsteam.co.uk, Crown Copyright 2009.
http://www.flickr.com/photos/londonsummit/3409198226/

that thin film of atmosphere which affords the greenhouse effect, proportionally no thicker than the skin on an apple. Gordon Brown (front row dead center) seems awestruck as if realizing that collectively they can define the pathways of life and death on Earth. In contrast, Luiz Inácio Lula da Silva (to his right) is distracted and oblivious. Who among them should step up? It is only fitting that the Head of State of the worst polluting country be called on the carpet. He is the tall thin man in the red silk tie with a winning smile (Figure C.2). Our flight of fantasy is reason for hope. JUSTICE, LIMITS, SURVIVAL substitutes for STABILITY, GROWTH, JOBS. Mercilessly, the fantasy flips back to its original position. Reason for despair is the reality.

Barack Obama tells a world audience that joblessness rates released in the US that very day were the highest in twenty-six years. He waxes that "so many have lost so much" and wanes how countries did not react to a similar crisis in the 1930s. "Today we've learned the lessons of history." Despite extraordinary oratory skill, the content of the speech was pure cowboy economics. The nadir was reached with "...I believe that we must put an end to the bubble-and-bust economy that has stood in the way of sustained growth...."[16]

Ironically, the pursuit of "sustained growth" guarantees a "bubble-and-bust economy." The term "sustained growth" is a "thunderous oxymoron"[17] and reveals a shocking ignorance of how compounding interest works. As an aside, it also demonstrates the abject failure of "ecological economics" as a school of thought to penetrate the top echelons of power. Combining "sustained" with "growth" confuses the public with "sustainable development" which is the antithesis of "sustained growth." Was Obama's intent to deceive? Such a question may seem unduly harsh on a new president who inherited the worst mess of any president in US history. Indeed, reasonable people should grant heads of state a certain number of indulgences for saying stupid things off the cuff. However, "sustained growth" was not said off the cuff. Everything on that stage, including the color of the stage itself – perhaps even the ties and turban – were vetted by experts in public relations. Recalling the treatise of French philosopher Jacques Ellul, the Summit was unequivocally a "propaganda operation."[18] The G-20 wanted to drum three messages into our globalized heads "STABILITY, GROWTH, JOBS" and the ethereal teleprompter would minimize any deviance from the script. The word "sustained" joined to "growth" is reason for despair.

The supreme lesson among all the "lessons of history" is that collapse ensues when a society overshoots its limits. Again, this is not new. Shortly after the publication of Hardin's "The Tragedy of the Commons" in 1968, the Club of Rome commissioned systems scientists and computer modelers to simulate the consequences of a rapidly populating Earth and the possibilities for sustainable feedback loops.[19] In 1972, Donella H. Meadows et al. published *The Limits to Growth* and its findings were widely cited in both the academic literature and the popular press.[20] Nevertheless, its central message, evident in its very title, was unassimilated into the body politic. Tragically, science would remain an uninvited guest in world politics from the mid-1960s onward. Any belated recognition of this intellectual history must support the argument advanced by Alan S. Blinder: wrench public policy from elected officials and place it within the realm of a technocracy.

With the passage of the "American Clean Energy and Security Act" (H.R. 2454) on 26 June 2009, the Blinder recommendation could not be more *au courant*. At first blush, the bill is reason for hope. In the clash among powerful lobbies, climate change was recognized and cap-and-trade emerged as the policy tool. Scratch a bit deeper and there is much more reason for despair. The bill passed by an incredibly slim margin (219–212). Had just 1% of the congressional representatives shifted position, it would have failed. Only eight Republicans (the opposition party) voted for it and some forty-four Democrats joined the 168 Republicans against. In other words, had the Republicans maintained their much vaunted party discipline, the bill would have been defeated. Paul Krugman summed up the social psychology of the debate on the floor of the House of Representatives:

[Y]ou didn't see people who've thought hard about a crucial issue, and are trying to do the right thing. What you saw, instead, were people who show no sign of being interested in the truth...Representative Paul Broun of Georgia [declared] that climate change is nothing but a 'hoax' that has been 'perpetrated out of the scientific community.' I'd call this a crazy conspiracy theory, but doing so would actually be unfair to crazy conspiracy theorists. After all, to believe that global warming is a hoax you have to believe in a vast cabal consisting of thousands of scientists – a cabal so powerful that it has managed to create false records on everything from global temperatures to Arctic sea ice. Yet Mr. Broun's declaration was met with applause.[21]

The night before the vote, rust belt lobbyists added a provision that requires that the president impose a "border adjustment" – doublespeak for tariffs – on goods from countries that did not limit their greenhouse gas emissions by the year 2020. Like a cliff-hanger novel, the compromise was an unexpected twist and unexpectedly, it is reason for hope. From the theory of second best, aka "leakages," the provision is a countervailing distortion that can enhance the global efficiency of stabilizing atmospheric carbon. The year 2020 is sufficiently far into the future that the poor carbon-rich countries, with the aid of North-to-South payments, can pass through the bottleneck of a cowboy economy and accept the limits of cap-and-trade. But like all cheap romance novels, the twists and turns just keep on coming. Reason for despair is Obama's opposition to the provision.[22] Now no longer a candidate for president, he no longer opposes free trade agreements with weak environmental standards. DITTO for his position on auctioning off the carbon emission permits;

Obama now favors giving them to big business. No doubt the flip-flops were to secure bipartisan support for H.R. 2454. As reported in *The New York Times*, "…the legislation, a patchwork of compromises, falls far short of what many European governments and environmentalists have said is needed to avert the worst effects of global warming."[23] In keeping with Orwell, Obama trumpets the bill as a "bold and necessary step"[24] rather than a pusillanimous and disappointing half-measure.

What is good for the goose is good for the gander. The economics of the Yasuní-ITT Initiative rests on the *realpolitik* that poor carbon-rich countries will extract their fuel reserves if not paid to do otherwise. The tortured text of the "American Clean Energy and Security Act" rests on the *realpolitik* of Big Oil and Coal. In a press interview about the bill, Obama made sense of his own contradictory positions. "I think legitimately people want the framework in place and for us to make strong, steady, gradual progress, as opposed to trying to shoot for the moon and not being able to get anything done."[25] Such *realpolitik* is also shared by Al Gore "This bill doesn't solve every problem, but passage today means that we build momentum for the debate coming up in the Senate and negotiations for the treaty talks in December which will put in place a global solution to the climate crisis. There is no backup plan."[26]

Whatever bill ultimately passes the US Senate, its dynamics suggests an analogy which is a good way to end this book and begin reflection on the Yasuní-ITT Initiative. A man is diagnosed with cancer and the oncologist orders treatment. The patient waits and waits and waits. He is not suicidal but thinks "What does this doctor *really* know?" Over the next few weeks, he gets a second opinion and then a third opinion…they are all the same: a chemotherapeutic cocktail. Meanwhile, the cancer is spreading. Begrudgingly, the man begins taking the medicine. But pride mixes with fear and he takes just one third of the prescribed dose. What does the oncologist say? It depends on the personality of the oncologist. A hopeful one will urge the patient to follow the full regime. A discouraged one will level with the man "either you follow the full regime or don't bother taking anything." The dishonest one says "those side-effects aren't all that bad …"

Group suicide is the banality of evil and we have no choice but to be hopeful. The economics of the Yasuní-ITT Initiative is part of the cocktail.

Appendix
ANNOTATED YOUTUBE FILMOGRAPHY
A Collaborative Effort
Janny Robles

Henry Jenkins, Director of the Program of Comparative Media Studies at the Massachusetts Institute of Technology, imagines a new form of academic unit where Departments "operat[e] more like YouTube or Wikipedia, allowing for the rapid deployment of scattered expertise and the dynamic reconfiguration of fields." He calls it the "YouNiversity" where "we don't so much need a faculty as we need an intellectual network." The methodology lies in an analogy. "Much as engineering students learn by taking apart machines and putting them back together, many of these teens learned how media work by taking their culture apart and remixing it."[1] The filmography of *The Economics of the Yasuní Initiative* adopts the spirit of the YouNiversity.

As an assistant to Professor Vogel since 2005 – the year that YouTube went online – I have seen first-hand how video-sharing has reconfigured learning. YouTube economizes the most precious of all resources: time. One can quickly gain familiarity with a diversity of topics through clips, some less than a minute long, and then lever those clips into classroom discussion. Nevertheless, the rich reservoir of the YouTube site raises the most mundane of questions: which clips?

Like so many questions in economics, the answer depends on the purpose. The purpose of *The Economics of the Yasuní Initiative* is to persuade the public that the carbon-rich-but-economically-poor countries must be compensated to get them through the bottleneck of a cowboy economy. Entertainment is key to persuasion. In other words, the clips that appear in this filmography should not only enrich our understanding but also entertain. For problems that afford no technical solution – like climate fluctuations and transformation – we must get the discussion going about "mutual coercion, mutually agreed upon."[2] To do so, Vogel believes we need a different school of economic thought and the school he suggests is *not* ecological economics.[3] He looks to the humanities and recommends "ecocriticism" which is defined as "the field of enquiry that analyzes and promotes works of art which raise moral questions about human interactions with nature, while also motivating audiences to live within a limit that will be binding over generations."[4]

The question persists: which clips? YouTube can quickly overwhelm any novice and some sort of filter is needed. Vogel has asked his students to research the YouTube site and identify those clips which best capture some essential point in each of the chapters and then draft a 100 word summary of the clip. In the division of labor, my job was to vet the onslaught of submissions and, through a group discussion with referees, cull them. Our favorites are listed here, chapter by chapter, with the student author duly identified.

Although the assignment seemed straightforward to us, the students were confused. We needed an example. Thinking about the subtitle *Climate Change as if Thermodynamics Mattered* and surfing the YouTube site, I quickly found *The Story of Stuff*. With a bit more surfing, I also found an excellent annotation which has served as the model for student authors writing their own summaries:

The Story of Stuff with Anne Leonard. Tides Foundation, Funders WorkGroup for Sustainable Production and Consumption and Free Range Studios. http://www.youtube.com/watch?v=OqZMTY4V7Ts

From its extraction through sale, use and disposal, all the stuff in our lives affects communities at home and abroad, yet most of this is hidden from view. 'The Story of Stuff' is a 20-minute, fast-paced, fact-filled look at the underside of our production and consumption patterns. 'The Story of Stuff' exposes the connections between a huge number of environmental and social issues, and calls us together to create a more sustainable and just world. It'll teach you something, it'll make you laugh, and it just may change the way you look at all the stuff in your life forever.[5]

By The Open Vision Community (an Educational Resource for the New Age)

Foreword: Yasuní: The New Economics of Planet Earth

The Beginning of the Future. Fuse Films.
http://www.youtube.com/watch?v=QRlTVJjUIlU
From the steps of the Butler Library at Columbia University to the steps of power in Washington, D.C., Graciela Chichilnisky, UNESCO Chair of Mathematics and Economics, explains why sustainable development must move from theory into practice. The format is a student-led interview. Interspersed are images which illustrate the overarching thesis: planet Earth is undergoing a "global tragedy of the commons." Solutions exist that must begin with legislation and the camera zooms in on the US Congress. The clip ends with a clear explanation of the unfairness of global warming and disturbing photos to which the viewer must not look away.

By Sylvia González

Introduction

Playa FOAM [Styrofoam Beach]. Haimo Ecofilms.
http://www.youtube.com/watch?v=zC9uKDPzw5A
We are a long way from Adam Smith's pin factory. On the beach in Puerto Rico, Joseph Henry Vogel measures trash. He explains how to estimate the cost of cleaning the beach transect by transect. The views are stunning. What bothers Vogel most is not the soiled diapers, not the discarded condoms, and not even the hypodermic needles! It is Styrofoam. The cost of picking up itsy bitsy Styrofoam is insurmountable. The policy solution is to ban the stuff. The clip is unrehearsed and we have a glimpse into the mind of an economist who insists that thermodynamics matters.

By Josué Sánchez-Manzanillo

Chapter 1:   Thermodynamics:
              The Language Chosen Defines the Debate

Toxic Linfen, China – The World's Most Polluted City – Pt1. WWW.VBS.TV
http://www.youtube.com/watch?v/ =c9tJNcktVWc&feature/=fvst
    Although not mentioned once, the video is all about "scale" and "sink."
    Fueled by coal, China grows pell-mell and the scale overwhelms the sink.
    Linfen has the dubious distinction of being the world's most polluted city.
    "Free trade" is the enabler and globalization, the driver. Thinking
    thermodynamically, one understands how "production" is ultimately the
    transformation of energy and material into the sink. Pity the reporter who
    relates that breathing the air in one day is equivalent to smoking three
    packages of cigarettes. And please consider the people of Linfen on your
    next trip to the shopping mall or...the voting booth.

                                                            By Nora Alvarez

Oil Addiction. Kenneth Cole Productions.
http://www.youtube.com/watch?v=EOm18c5Btiw&feature=related
    Can 4.5 billion years be compressed into a video of 4.5 minutes? It can
    from the viewpoint of fossil fuels. Out of the swirling clouds of an infant
    solar system emerge Earth, primitive life, dinosaurs, and finally the human
    technology to access the accumulated detritus of the past: oil drills. Fuel
    quickly gets translated into skyrocketing human populations and all
    their fuel-driven accoutrements. The longest ride of the roller coaster
    are the crises *du jour* in 2008 (imagine the update for 2009?). No longer
    "America, love it or Leave it," the video ends with "America, love it and
    fix it."

                                                            By Jomara A. Laboy

Chapter 2:   The Tragedy of the Commons:
              A Class of Problems that Has no Technical Solution

Animation: Climate Change, Energy & Action. WWF.ORG.BR
http://www. youtube.com/watch?v=_s9dxc_jVlY
    Blackboard economics gives way to whiteboard creativity. Easy to upload,
    one sees production and consumption morph into sustainability. It is wise
    to freeze some frames and analyze the action. The first is an Earth where
    built structures sprout all along the circumference. No frontier exists. The
    caption reads 23 billion tons of CO_2 per year. Six and a half billion people
    shed their one billion cars and opt for mass transit, bicycles and walking.
    Belching factories give way to windmills and land reclamation.
    Incandescent light bulbs are out and solar panels are in. Solutions, both
    technical and non-technical, beautifully intermingle.

                                                            By Haniel Velez Rosario

Gas Prices, Gas Gouging, Peak Oil, Elasticity, Supply Demand. Local Future Network.
http://www.youtube.com/watch?v=T7vGDwGLU7s&feature=
PlayList& =9598583CA57C189D&playnext=1&index=40

> Listen to the monotone and imagine sitting through ECON101.
> Nevertheless, the graphs explain well the dynamism of shifting demand
> and supply curves. If one were able to predict how both curves move at
> specific moments, one could make a killing in crude oil trading, selling or
> buying options, short or long. But the slightest miscalculation would spell
> *ADIEU* to the dreams of early retirement in the French Riviera. An oddity:
> what does the red supply curve mean when it crosses into the negative
> zone of production? I think it's an error. I daresay economics is not easy
> even for economists.
>
> By Miriam Lopez-Medel

Chapter 3: The Willful Ignorance of *Realpolitik*:
Market Failure or Cost-shifting Success?

Negative Externalities. St. Lawrence College, Athens, Greece.
http://www.youtube.com/watch?v=S0lH4GEFy1o&feature=PlayList&p=
0C165813BDCBAF9A&index=4

> Language can be a mechanism of exclusion. The video begins with a
> definition of externality and its economic synonyms, external or social
> costs. Immediately, the audience is channeled to speak in *economese*.
> On the whiteboard, the narrator draws supply and demand and then adds
> social costs. The model is meant to be generic and therein lies the rub. Can
> violent climate fluctuations be accommodated with the same economics
> as second-hand smoke or traffic jams? Is the "externality" a misnomer
> for a centrality? Most importantly, does the language exclude the public
> from discussing self-imposed limits through "mutual coercion, mutually
> agreed upon?"
>
> By Gamaliel Lamboy Rodríguez

Coal: The Human Cost. Greenpeace Beijing.
http://www.youtube.com/watch?v=MwTYVhsQYw4

> Even "cost-shifting success" does not do justice for the victims who pay the
> ultimate price. We hear first hand accounts of the horrors wrought by the
> coal that drives Chinese manufactures. Collapse is no metaphor when
> talking about mines. The stories have largely eluded the mainstream press,
> which is embedded in a system to buy, buy, buy the "cheap" Chinese
> exports. To translate into *economese* the death and destruction as "market
> failure" is not just Orwellian, it is obscene. Perhaps the Yasuní-ITT
> Initiative will serve as a pilot project which helps China through its own
> bottleneck of a cowboy economy.
>
> By Marta Gisela Romero Martínez

Chapter 4:   "The General Theory of Second Best:"
A Rigorous Justification for an Intuitively Just Proposal

Carbon Trading Simplified. Brown Hat Media.
http://www.youtube.com/watch?v=YfQyPl6BkP4&feature=related

Simplicity requires a stepwise development in explaining any complex system. Carbon trading is baffling because an impatient audience wants to get to the bottom line – markets – without understanding each step along the way. In a lovely and mellifluous voice, the narrator begins with the geographic distribution of emissions worldwide, represented in bar diagrams. She explains how the Clean Development Mechanism of the Kyoto Protocol reduces global emissions. The trade is illustrated through some simple calculations. However, absent among the projects financed through such trading (image at 2:06) is keeping the oil underground. By the logic of Yasuní-ITT Initiative, it should be included.

By Zulimar Lucena

Cap, Trade, Grow. Op-Ad Media and Planet Vox.
http://www.youtube.com/watch?v=oZauAFqd1Q8

Despite hype to the contrary, "cap and trade" is conservative. The atmosphere is the latest application of market economics. Various commentators explore the reality that the skies are an "open sewer." The first is no less than a four-star US Air Force General. Even W. has a cameo appearance. Clips of Bush *père* signing the first "cap and trade" legislation over SO_2 shows that the idea is nothing new. The solutions showcased are all technological. What happens when growth swamps the carbon savings? By the theory of second best, the title is wrong. It should be "cap, trade, and manage."

By Gianfranco Tiralongo

Chapter 5:   Through the Bottleneck of a Cowboy Economy:
Financing Shovel-ready Projects

[Channel 4 News] Population Explosion Causes Poverty. NewsRevue's Channel.
http://www.youtube.com/watch?v=LFgb1BdPBZo

Some news stories never become dated. Overpopulation is one of them. Nigeria is an oil-producing country which nevertheless suffers abject poverty. Starvation in the countryside propels migration to the capital and the crowding in Lagos defies words. One must see the images to understand the tragedy. Pan-shots of its mega-slum are anchored by statistics of population growth. Through the close-ups, one sees the squalor: open sewage ditches and rubbish everywhere, including toxic drums and hospital wastes. An interview with Basi Ratza Cura, an 11-year old orphan, is not an anecdote. The deprivation she lives is lived daily by millions worldwide.

By Jonathan Ortiz

Humans! Animation. Aniboom History Channel.
http://www.youtube.com/watch?v=GKEAXOnogZU&feature=fvw
   Black humor can be effective, especially in cartoons. A different metaphor for the cowboy economy is scabies. The victim is a green and smiling planet. On its temple, at about the location of Los Angeles, is a worrisome black spot. Under the magnifying glass, we discover that the affliction is humans. The scabies spread fast as the planet spins. Every niche is colonized and destroyed. A drill is penetrating the floor of a pristine forest and oil gushes forth. Yasuní, anyone? In a mere geological second, the planet staggers and collapses. Cheek-to-jowl, the scabies rocket toward the next hapless planet.

By Stefanie Uriarte Naranjo

Conclusions: Reason for Hope and Despair

Simulation of Cancer Growth I. Kuscsik's Channel.
http://www.youtube.com/watch?v=xbWPTJRE4Kg&NR=1
   Just as small is beautiful, less can also be more. Stripped of sound and even of color, this 25 second video is powerful in its starkness. A cancer cell splits and continues splitting until the cells occupy the whole screen. And then what happens? If you cannot answer that question much less perceive the metaphor, see the video again until the answer becomes apparent. Would that the world leaders of the G-20 spend the 25 seconds to watch this clip! OK, some may have to see it again and again. Sustained growth is a delusion in pursuit of a tragedy.

By Dionisio Pérez

The Ecological Debt. Resist Network.
http://www.youtube.com/watch?v=xADa-bUuuOo&feature=
response_ watch
   The camera jumps a bit but the logic is steady. An unnamed British journalist interviews Canadian activist Naomi Klein. Mexican actor Gael García Bernal listens attentively. The topic is the carbon debt. Through such conversations, people will work out their own position regarding the correctness of the Yasuní-ITT Initiative and its potential for sustainable development. Ms. Klein comments "These countries are paying a higher price for emissions that they themselves did not produce. So it's a whole new way of doing math, it's a whole other way of thinking about economics." Ecuador has become the model.

By Stefan R. Klajbor

NOTES

Foreword

[1] Graciela Chichilnisky, "North South Trade and the Global Environment," *American Economic Review* 84 no. 4 (1994): 851–74.

[2] Graciela Chichilnisky and Geoffrey Heal, "Who Should Abate: An International Perspective," *Economic Letters*, Spring (1994): 443–49.

[3] See *World Bank* Report "The State and Trends of the Carbon Market" 2006, 2007 and 2008.

[4] Graciela Chichilnisky, "The Abatement of carbon emission in industrial and developing countries" in *The Economics of Climate Change*, T. Jones, ed (Paris: OECD, 1994), 159–70.

[5] See Graciela Chichilnisky and Geoffrey Heal, eds. *Environmental Markets: Equity and Efficiency* (New York: Columbia University Press, 2000); Chichilnisky, "North-South Trade"; Chichilnisky and Heal, "Who Should Abate?".

[6] Graciela Chichilnisky, *Development and Global Finance: The Case for an International Bank for Environmental Settlements* (New York: UNDP and UNESCO, 1976).

Introduction

[1] Oliver L. Phillips, et al., "Drought Sensitivity of the Amazon Rainforest," *Science* 323 no. 5919 (2009): 1344–1347.

[2] Nicholas Stern, *The Economics of Climate Change: The Stern Review* (New York: Cambridge, 2006), 657.

[3] Ibid, 1.

[4] Eperanza Martínez, "Dejar el crudo en tierra en el Yasuní: un reto a la coherencia," *Revista Tendencia* 9, marzo-abril 2009, 67–72.

[5] Though the proposal is officially known as The Yasuní-ITT Initiative, I have suppressed the acronym ITT in the title of this book. The acronym ties the tongue and limits audience receptivity. Economics is a rhetorical enterprise.

[6] The language used in the Declaration of the Fifth Summit of the Americas in Port of Spain, Trinidad and Tobago, April 2009. Online: http://www.summit-americas.org/V_Summit/decl_comm_pos_en.pdf (accessed 27 October 2009).

Chapter 1

[1] Linda Blimes and Joseph Stiglitz, *The Three Trillion Dollar War* (New York: W. W. Norton Press, 2008).

[2] Paul A. Samuelson and William D. Nordhaus, *ECONOMICS*, 18th ed. (New York: McGraw-Hill, 2005), Figure 2–1, 29.

[3] Ibid, 36.

[4] Robert L. Heilbroner, *The Worldly Philosophers*, 2nd ed. (New York: Simon and Schuster, 1972), 15.

[5] Ibid, 27.

[6] J. T. Houghton, G. J. Jenkins and J. J. Ephraums, eds., *Climate Change: The IPCC Assessment* (UK: Cambridge University Press, 1990).

[7] Kenneth E. Boulding, *The Economics of the Coming Spaceship Earth* (Baltimore, MD: The Johns Hopkins Press, 1966).

[8] Thomas S. Kuhn, *The Structure of Scientific Revolutions* (Chicago: University of Chicago Press, 1962). For an online study guide: http://des.emory.edu/mfp/Kuhn.html (accessed 26 October 2009).

[9] Garrett Hardin, "The Tragedy of the Commons," *Science* 162 (1968): 1243–1248. Online: http://dieoff.org/page95.htm (accessed 26 October 2009); Paul R. Ehrlich, *The Population Bomb* (New York: Ballantine Books, 1968).

[10] George S. Howard, "The Tragedy of Maximization," *The Ecopsychology Institute*, 1997. Online: http://ecopsychology.athabascau.ca/1097/index.htm #politics (accessed 26 October 2009).

[11] The two examples are a small sample of a rich compendium entitled "Reagan Quotes: Was he really that dumb?" Online: http://www.geocities.com/thereaganyears/reaganquotes.htm (accessed 26 October 2009).

[12] "For the more one looks into the origins of the current disaster, the clearer it becomes that the key wrong turn – the turn that made crisis inevitable – took place in the early 1980s, during the Reagan years." Paul Krugman, "Reagan Did It," *The New York Times*, 1 June 2009, A21.

[13] Alice Rivlin, founding Director of the Congressional Budget Office (CBO), interviewed in June 1997 by David Levy, Vice President of The Federal Reserve Bank of Minneapolis, responds "Probably the high point of my name recognition on streets and in airports was at the beginning of the Reagan administration. I was at that time director of the Congressional Budget Office and testified a great deal on the Reagan budget. We warned that the Reagan budget would create high deficits. We were right. But

actually we didn't know the half of it. The deficits were much worse than anything predicted by the CBO." Online: http://www.minneapolisfed.org/publications_papers/pub_display.cfm?id=3638 (accessed 26 October 2009).

[14] William D. Nordhaus, *Managing the Global Commons: The Economics of Climate Change* (MIT Press, 1994); William D. Nordhaus and Joseph Boyer, *Warming the World: Economic Models of Global Warming* (Cambridge, Mass: MIT Press, 2000).

[15] David Leonhardt, "A Battle over the Costs of Global Warming," *The New York Times*, 21 February 2007.

[16] Martin Luther King's "Beyond Viet Nam" speech delivered at the Riverside Church on 4 April 1967. Online: http://www.americanrhetoric.com/speeches/mlkatimetobreaksilence.htm (accessed 26 October 2009).

[17] Paul Krugman, "Same Old Party," *The New York Times*, 8 October 2007.

[18] Norway is the notable exception which may have something to do with not being a member of the European Union.

[19] Susan George, *A Fate Worse than Debt* (London: Penguin, 1988).

[20] Agenda 21 UN Department of Economic and Social Affairs. Online: http://www.un.org/esa/dsd/agenda21/ (accessed 26 October 2009).

[21] Paul Schilpp, *Albert Einstein, Philosopher-Scientist: The Library of Living Philosophers Volume VII* (Chicago: Open Court, 1998), 33.

[22] Eric D. Schneider and Dorion Sagan, *Into The Cool: Energy Flow, Thermodynamics, and Life* (Chicago and London: University of Chicago Press, 2005), 138.

[23] E. F. Schumacher, *Small is Beautiful* (New York: Harper & Row, 1973), 54.

[24] Herman E. Daly, *Steady-State Economics*, 2nd ed. (Washington, D.C.: Island Press, 1991), xii.

[25] E. O. Wilson enthusiastically endorses ecological economics and laments that "[m]ost economists today, and all but the most politically conservative of their public interpreters, recognize very well that the world has limits and the human population cannot afford to grow much larger. They know that humanity is destroying biodiversity. They just don't like to spend a lot of time thinking about it." *The Future of Life* (New York: Vintage Books, 2002), 28.

[26] Nicholas Georgescu-Roegen, *The Entropy Law and the Economic Process* (Cambridge: Harvard University Press, 1971), 281.

[27] Garrett Hardin, *Living Within Limits* (New York: Oxford University Press, 1993), 60.

[28] Ibid, 57.

[29] Hardin gives due credit to Boulding, op. cit.

[30] Perhaps I am being overly generous. "Already at the end of the 18th century, [William Wordsworth's] thinking uncovers possible roots of the modern environmental crisis." Christian Becker, Malte Faber, Kirsten Hertel, Reiner Manstetten, "Malthus vs. Wordsworth: Perspectives on Humankind, Nature, and Economy. A Contribution to the History and Foundations of Ecological Economics" *Ecological Economics* 53 (2005): 299–310, 300. As the quote from *Hamlet* in the epigraph makes clear, even by the 16th century, air pollution was not unknown.

[31] Paul R. Ehrlich and Anne H. Ehrlich, *The Dominant Animal* (Washington, DC: Island Press, 2009), 190.

[32] The assumption that capital can always substitute for resources is highlighted in the critique from ecological economics. Less mentioned is the thermodynamic fact that nothing can substitute for the sink.

[33] Graciela Chichilnisky and Geoffrey Heal, eds., *Environmental Markets: Equity and Efficiency* (New York: Columbia University Press, 2000).

[34] Jeff Goodell, "Capital Pollution Solution," *The New York Times Magazine*, 30 July 2006.

[35] Brian R. Copeland and M. Scott Taylor, "Free Trade and Global Warming: A Trade Theory View of the Kyoto Protocol," *NBER Working Paper No. W7657*, April 2000.

[36] However, a caveat is in order. Multi-tasking is usually a misnomer for task-switching which is fraught with hazards. "Bad at Multi-tasking. Blame your Brain," *National Public Radio*, 16 October 2008. Online: http://www.npr.org/templates/story/story.php?storyId=95784052&ft=1&f=1021 (accessed 26 October 2009)

[37] "Kid's Page," *Pew Center on Global Climate Change*. Online: http://www.pewclimate.org/global-warming-basics/kidspage.cfm#Q3 (accessed 12 April 2009).

[38] *An Introduction to Early Greek Philosophy*, trans. John Mansley Robinson (Boston: Houghton Mifflin Company, 1968), Fragment 5.15, 91 and Fragment 5.10, 89.

[39] Eric J. Chaisson, *Cosmic Evolution: The Rise of Complexity in Nature* (Cambridge: Harvard University Press, 2001), 59.

[40] Ilya Prigogine and Isabelle Stengers, *Order Out of Chaos* (New York: Bantam Books, 1984).

[41] E. O. Wilson, *Consilience* (New York: Alfred A. Knopf, 1998), 4.

[42] Heilbroner, op. cit., 12.

Chapter 2

[1] Garrett Hardin, "The Tragedy of the Commons," *Science* 162 (1968): 1243–1248. Online: http://dieoff.org/page95.htm (accessed 26 October 2009).

[2] Hardin uses the words "technical" and "technological" synonymously in "The Tragedy." One assumes the alternating choice of words was to avoid monotony in exposition. Because "technical" may also connote rigor in argumentation, the reader must be careful not to equivocate.

[3] Jeffrey D. Sachs, "Keys to Climate Protection," *Scientific American,* April 2008. Online: http://www.scientificamerican.com/article.cfm?id=technological-keys-to-climate-protection-extended (accessed 26 October 2009).

[4] Ibid.

[5] Hardin, op. cit.

[6] Sachs, op. cit., "ls_1955" at 7:06AM on 06/19/08.

[7] For a comprehensive critique against "geo-engineering," see the website of Erosion, Technology, Concentration. Online: http://www.etcgroup.org/en/ (accessed 26 October 2009). Even the mainstream news media reports the legitimate fears. Matthew L. Wald, "Refitted to Bury Emissions, Plant Draws Attention," *The New York Times*, 22 September 2009, A1.

[8] Andrew Revkin, "A Shift in the Debate over Global Warming" *The New York Times*, Week in Review, 6 April 2008.

[9] Garrett Hardin, *Living Within Limits* (New York: Oxford University Press, 1993), 299.

[10] Garrett Hardin, "The Tragedy of the Commons," *Science* 162 (1968): 1243–1248.

[11] The lesson of Rapa Nui (Easter Island) is important. With ingenious techniques, the ancestral populations exhausted one resource after another to construct the 800 some *maoi* (stone statues) that they ultimately toppled. Jared Diamond, *Collapse: How Societies Choose to Fail or Succeed* (New York: Viking Press, 2005).

[12] Blake Alcott, "Jevon's Paradox," *Ecological Economics* 54(1), July 2005, 9–21.

[13] Anil Argawal and Sunita Narain, "The Fridge, The Greenhouse, and the Carbon Sink," *The New Internationalist* 230, April 1992. Online: http://www.newint.org/issue230/fridge.htm (accessed 26 October 2009).

[14] The title and subtitle of a front page article from *USA Today* say it all. Calum MacLeod, "China's Car Sales Boom, Reshaping a Way of Life: Thirst for Mobility Could Help US Automakers," 15 June 2009, 1A–2A.

[15] John Vidal and David Adam, "China Overtakes US as World´s Biggest CO2 Emitter," 19 June 2007. Online: http://www.guardian.co.uk/environment/2007/jun/19/china.usnews (accessed 26 October 2009).

[16] Victoria M. Markham, "US Population, Energy, & Climate Change" (CEP 2008), 4. Online: http://www.cepnet.org/documents/USPopulationEnergy andClimateChangeReportCEP.pdf (accessed 26 October 2009).

[17] UNFCCC Subsidiary Body for Scientific and Technical Advice, Thirteenth Session, Lyon, 11–15 September 2000. Online: http://www.ccsr.u-tokyo.ac.jp/unfccc3/pdfs/unfccc.int/resource/docs/2000/sbsta/misc08a01.pdf (accessed 26 October 2009).

[18] Natural Resources Canada. Online: http://carbon.cfs.nrcan.gc.ca/definitions_e.html (accessed 26 October 2009).

[19] Perhaps sensitive to the fallacy of equivocation, the journalist Elisabeth Rosenthal eschews the Kyoto language of "carbon sink" and correctly deploys "carbon absorption potential," "In Brazil, Paying Farmers to Let the Trees Stand," *The New York Times*, 22 August 2009, A1.

[20] Philip B. Duffy and Kenneth G. Caldeira, "Tracing the Role of Carbon Dioxide in Global Warming," *Science and Technology*, March 1998. Online: https://www.llnl.gov/str/Duffy.html (accessed 26 October 2009).

[21] Paul R. Ehrlich and Anne H. Ehrlich, *The Dominant Animal* (Washington, D.C.: Island Press, 2009), 293.

[22] Paul A. Samuelson, *The Foundations of Economic Analysis* (Cambridge: Harvard University Press, 1947).

[23] Notable exceptions exist. Deirdre McCloskey, *The Rhetoric of Economics*, 2nd ed. (Madison: The University of Wisconsin Press, 1998).

[24] For a concise definition of the fallacy of equivocation, see *Blackwell Online*: http://www.blackwellreference.com/public/tocnode?id=g9781405106795_chunk_g97814051067957_ss1-18 (accessed 26 October 2009).

[25] Garrett Hardin, *Exploring New Ethics for Survival* (Baltimore, Maryland: Penguin Books, 1972).

[26] Ibid, 66–70.

[27] William Stanley Jevons, *The Coal Question* (London: MacMillan and Co., 1866). Online: http://www.eoearth.org/article/The_Coal_Question_(e-book) (accessed 26 October 2009).

[28] "Beyond reasonable doubt" is a gross understatement. As Tim Flannery documents "[The IPCC reports] carry weight with the media and government precisely because they represent a consensus view. If the IPCC says something, you had better believe it – and then allow for the likelihood that things are far worse than it says they are." *The Weathermakers* (New York: Grove Press, 2005), 246.

[29] *United Nations Framework Convention on Climate Change, Changes in GHG emissions from 1990 to 2004 for Annex 1 Parties.* Online: http://unfccc.int/files/essential_background/background_publications_htmlpdf/application/pdf/ghg_table_06.pdf (accessed 26 October 2009).

[30] *CPB, Netherlands Bureau for Economic Policy Analysis, the Netherlands* Decomposing Carbon Leakage: An Analysis of the Kyoto Protocol. Online: http://www.iiasa.ac.at/Research/ECS/june99/abstracts/bollen1.pdf (accessed on Oct. 28, 2009).

[31] Sergey V Paltsev. "The Kyoto Protocol: Regional and Sectoral Contributions to the Carbon Leakage", *The Energy Journal*, vol 22, no. 4. Online: http://web.mit.edu/paltsev/www/pubs/ej2001.pdf and http://info.worldbank.org/etools/docs/voddocs/230/425/kyoto_leak.pdf (accessed 26 October 2009).

[32] Nicholas Stern, *The Economics of Climate Change: The Stern Review* (New York: Cambridge, 2006), 618.

[33] The "Memorial" in "Nobel Memorial Prize in Economics," albeit cumbersome, is neverthless less so than the correct name "Bank of Sweden Prize in Economic Sciences in Memory of Alfred Nobel." To say a "Nobel Prize in Economics" is a misleading short-hand that the Nobel Foundation does not use in the intralinks to the top bar of its homesite. Online: http://nobelprize.org/nobel_prizes/economics/laureates/ (accessed 26 October 2009).

[34] Stern, op. cit.

[35] It is absent in Paul A. Samuelson and William D. Nordhaus, *ECONOMICS* 18th ed. (New York: McGraw-Hill, 2005).

[36] Richard G. Lipsey, "Reflections on the General Theory of Second Best on its Golden Jubilee", *International Tax and Public Finance* 14 no. 4, August 2007. Online: http://www.gmu.edu/centers/publicchoice/SummerInstitute/papers08/lipsey%20wed.pdf (accessed 26 October 2009).

[37] Ibid.

[38] Joseph Henry Vogel, *Genes for Sale* (New York: Oxford University Press, 1994), 101.

[39] Joseph Henry Vogel, *Privatisation as a Conservation Policy* (Melbourne, CIRCIT, 1992), 111.

[40] Hardin, "The Tragedy."

[41] David Brooks, "The End of Philosophy," *The New York Times*, 6 April 2009, A29.

[42] Franz de Waals, *Primates and Philosophers: How Morality Evolved* (Princeton: Princeton University Press, 2006).

[43] Choice of words in translation can color the impact and lead to an unintended "moral snap judgment." I have translated the passage from

Spanish choosing those words that would most highlight what I believe to be Correa's overarching intention – fairness.

[44] Hardin's quotes *Situation Ethics* in "The Tragedy."

[45] "The members of the Group of Eight, or G-8, are Canada, France, Germany, Italy, Japan, Russia, the United Kingdom, and the United States." Summit 2009. Online: http://www.g8italia2009.it/G8/Home/Summit/Partecipanti/G8-G8_Layout_locale-1199882116809_PaesiG8.htm (accessed 26 October 2009).

[46] New Economics Foundation, *Economics as if People and the Planet Matter*, Principle 3, 6. Online:http://www.neweconomics.org/content/behavioural-economics (accessed 26 October 2009).

[47] Vanessa Baird, "Endgame in the Amazon," *The New Internationalist*, July 2008, 4–10.

[48] E. O. Wilson, *The Future of Life* (New York: Vintage Books, 2002), 23.

[49] PETROECUADOR, MEM 0207, powerpoint presentation, February 2007, "Evaluación económica, producción anticipada," slide 23.

[50] Mark Engler and Nadia Martinez, "Harken vs Costa Rica: US companies employ blackmail in "free trade" with Central America," *The Guardian* 1186, 9 June 2004.

[51] Based on 2000 and 2001 data, Costa Rica was within the category of High Human Development in the Human Development Index (HDI), ranking 43rd of 53 countries. Ecuador was in Medium Human Development, ranking 93rd of the 137 in that lower category. *Human Development Report 2002: Deepening Democracy in a Fragmented World* (New York: UNDP and Oxford University Press, 2002), 53. Online: http://hdr.undp.org/en/media/HDR_2002_EN_Complete.pdf (accessed 26 October 2009).

Chapter 3

[1] Others include "Big Brother," "newspeak," "doublethink," and derivatives like "groupthink."

[2] William Lutz, "Fourteen Years of Doublespeak," *The English Journal* 77: 3 (March 1988), 40–42, 40.

[3] *The Quarterly Review of Doublespeak*, 23 July 2002, ygfperson. Online: http://cboard.cprogramming.com/brief-history-cprogramming-com/22211-quarterly-review-doublespeak.html (accessed 26 October 2009).

[4] "Bush Administration Terrorism Memos," *The New York Times*, 3 March 2009. Online:http://documents.nytimes.com/bush-administration-terrorism-memos?scp=1&sq=bush%20terrorism%20memos&st=cse#p=1 (accessed 26 October 2009).

[5] Nicholas Stern, *The Economics of Climate Change: The Stern Review* (New York: Cambridge, 2006), xv.

[6] Defined as "politics based on practical and material factors rather than on theoretical or ethical objectives," *Merriam-Webster*. Online: http://www.merriam-webster.com/dictionary/realpolitik (accessed 26 October 2009).

[7] Stern, op. cit., 27.

[8] Ibid.

[9] Ibid.

[10] Karl Popper, *Conjectures and Refutations* (London: Routledge, 1963).

[11] Joan Martinez-Alier and Martin O'Connor, "Distributional Issues: an Overview" in *Handbook of Environmental and Resource Economics*, J. van den Bergh, ed. (Cheltenham: Edward Elgar, 1999).

[12] Stern, op. cit., 27.

[13] Joan Martínez-Alier, letter to the editor, *The Economist*, 28 June 2007. Online: http://www.sosyasuni.org/en/News/Response-letter-to-the-Economist.html (accessed 26 October 2009).

[14] John Kenneth Galbraith, *American Capitalism: The Concept of Countervailing Power* (Boston: Houghton Mifflin, 1952).

[15] Marc Bousquet, *How the University Works: Higher Education and the Low Wage Nation* (New York: New York University Press, 2008); Frank Donoghue, *The Last Professors: The Corporate University and the Fate of the Humanities* (New York: Fordham University Press, 2008).

[16] Paul Krugman, "Crony Capitalism, USA," *The New York Times*, 15 January 2002 and "Harry, Louise, and Barack,"*The New York Times*, May 11, 2009.

[17] Jared Diamond, *Guns, Germs, and Steel* (New York: W. W. Norton, 1997), see Ch. 14, "From Egalitarianism to Kleptocracy."

[18] Robert L. Heilbroner, *The Worldly Philosophers*, 2nd ed. (New York: Simon and Schuster, 1972), 205–239.

[19] One thinks of Stephen J. Gould, Carl Sagan, and even Jared Diamond.

[20] Al Gore, *An Inconvenient Truth: The Planetary Emergency of Global Warming and What We Can Do About* (New York: Rodale, 2006).

[21] Ibid, 10.

[22] Gore lists the 132 nations that have ratified in blue and then the two that have not ratified in red, viz., Australia and the United States, ibid, 282–283.

[23] Gore qualifies the statistics a bit to show that they are based on large random samples, ibid, 262–263.

[24] Ibid, 264.

[25] Ibid, 227.

[26] Stern, op. cit., 605.

[27] Gore, op. cit., 165–167.

[28] Lisa Mintz Messinger, *Georgia O'Keefe* (London: Thames & Hudson, 1991), 45.

[29] Gore, op. cit. 9.

[30] Garrett Hardin, "The Tragedy of the Commons," *Science* 162 (1968): 1243–1248. Online: http://dieoff.org/page95.htm (accessed 26 October 2009).

[31] Ibid.

[32] Gore, op. cit. 263 foldout.

[33] Carl Sagan, *The Demon Haunted World: Science as a Candle in the Dark* (New York: Random House, 1995), 217.

[34] "Free to Choose TV Series by Milton Friedman." Online: http://miltonfriedman.blogspot.com/ (accessed 2 November 2009).

[35] Hardin, op. cit.

[36] J. S. Hacker, *The Great Risk Shift: The New Insecurity and the Decline of the American Dream* (New York: Oxford University Press, 2006); Carmen DeNavas-Wait, Bernadette D. Proctor, and Jessica C. Smith, *Income, Poverty,*

and Health Insurance Coverage in the United States: 2008 (Washington, D.C.: US Census Bureau, September 2009). Online: http://www.census.gov/prod/2009pubs/p60-236.pdf (accessed 26 October 2009).

[37] "Tent Cities." Online: http://www.youtube.com/watch?v=HVwG01-bogE (accessed 26 October 2009).

[38] Sadomasochists notwithstanding, the ethics of the rule seems inviolable. *Luke* 6:31, *The Bible*, New International Version. Admittedly, the Yasuní-ITT Initiative violates it by recognizing the *realpolitik* of an eye for an eye.

[39] Hardin, op. cit.

[40] Susan George, "Transforming the Global Economy: Solutions for a Sustainable World," *The Schumacher Lecture*, 6 October 2008. Online: http://www.tni.org/en/events/transforming-global-economy-solutions-sustainable-world (accessed 26 October 2009).

[41] Jeffrey D. Sachs, "Keys to Climate Protection," *Scientific American*, April 2008. Online: http://www.scientificamerican.com/article.cfm?id=technological-keys-to-climate-protection-extended (accessed 26 October 2009); Paul Krugman, "It's Easy Being Green," *The New York Times*, 24 September 2009, A29.

[42] US Census Bureau, 2006, *Income, Poverty, and Health Insurance Coverage in the United States: 2005*, 40. Online: http://www.census.gov/prod/2006pubs/p60-231.pdf (accessed 26 October 2009).

[43] Editorial, "The Forgotten Rich," *The New York Times*, 2 April 2009.

[44] If a 10% reduction from 45 to 35% yields $250 billion, then an increase from 45 to 100% would yield $1.375 trillion.

[45] Quoted in a paraphrase by Richard O'Connor, *The Oil Barons: Men of Greed and Grandeur* (Boston: Little, Brown, 1971), 47. Original quote in French "Le secret des grandes fortunes sans cause apparente est un crime oublié, parce qu'il a été proprement fait," *Le Père Goriot* (1835), Part II. Online: http://fr.wikisource.org/wiki/Le_P%C3%A8re_Goriot_-_II._L%27 entr%C3%A9e_dans_le_monde (accessed 26 October 2009).

[46] Keith Obermann, "Leona Helmsley shows her love for Trouble," Anchor, 'Countdown', MSNBC updated 6:09 p.m. CT, 29 August 2007. Online: http://www.msnbc.msn.com/id/20501749/ (accessed 26 October 2009).

[47] Thomas Mann, *Buddenbrooks: The Decline of a Family*, John E. Woods, trans. (New York: Random House, Inc, 1994, from German, 1901).

Chapter 4

[1] Prize in Economics: Robert W. Fogel and Douglass C. North. Online: http://nobelprize.org/nobel_prizes/economics/laureates/1993/index.html (accessed 26 October 2009).

[2] For an excellent online synopsis, complete with graphs: http://www.sjsu.edu/faculty/watkins/fogel.htm (accessed 26 October 2009).

[3] Robert William Fogel and Stanley L. Engerman, *Time on the Cross: The Economics of American Negro Slavery* (Lanham, MD: University Press of America, 1974), 261.

[4]   Adam Smith, *An Inquiry into the Nature and Causes of the Wealth of Nations* 1, "Introduction and Plan of Work," 5th ed., Edwin Cannan, ed (London: Methuen & Co., Ltd, 1904 first published 1776]). Online at: http://www.econlib.org/library/Smith/smWN1.html (accessed 26 October 2009).

[5]   The quotation marks are necessary to avoid doublespeak. Under natural law, slave owners were in fact thieves.

[6]   Frederick Douglass credits his master, Mr. Auld, for words that had an *unintended* effect that was "neither slight nor transitory. His iron sentences sunk deep into my heart, and stirred up not only my feelings into a sort of rebellion, but awakened within me a slumbering train of vital thought...'knowledge unfits a child to be a slave.'" *Autobiographies: Narrative of the Life; My Bondage and My Freedom; Life and Times*, Henry Louis Gates, Jr, ed (New York: Library of America, 1994), 118.

[7]   Claude F. Oubre, *Forty Acres and a Mule: The Freedmen's Bureau and Black Land Ownership* (Baton Rouge, LA: Louisiana State University Press, 1978); Eric Foner, *A Short History of Reconstruction, 1863–1877* (New York: Harper & Row, 1990).

[8]   Eric Foner, "What Will History Say? He's the Worst Ever" *The Washington Post*, 3 December 2006. Online: http://www.washingtonpost.com/wp-dyn/content/article/2006/12/01/AR2006120101509.html (accessed 27 October 2009).

[9]   William Faulkner, *Requiem for a Nun* (New York: Random House, 1951), 92. In the US presidential campaign speech "A More Perfect Union," Barack Obama not only misquoted but embellished. "As William Faulkner once wrote 'The past isn't dead and buried. In fact, it isn't even past.'" *The Wall Street Journal*, 18 March 2008. Online: http://blogs.wsj.com/washwire/2008/03/18/text-of-obamas-speech-a-more-perfect-union/ (accessed 26 October 2009).

[10] James McPherson, *Battle Cry of Freedom: The Civil War Era* (New York: Oxford University Press, 1988).

[11] James Hansen, "The Enemy of the Human Race," *SIERRA*, May/June 2009, 41.

[12] No analogy is perfect. Delaware was a slave state but not part of the Confederacy and Lincoln's Proclamation of Emancipation of 1 January 1863 did not apply to the slave-owning border states. Slavery ended in the US with the ratification of the Thirteenth Amendment on the 18th of December 1865.

[13] "Voluntary resignations" leads one to ask about the Orwellian inference, viz., "non-voluntary resignations" or the even more Orwellian "renuncias forzosas" [forced resignations].

[14] Richard G. Lipsey, "Reflections on the General Theory of Second Best on its Golden Jubilee," *International Tax and Public Finance* 14 (4), August 2007. Online: http://www.gmu.edu/centers/publicchoice/SummerInstitute/papers08/lipsey%20wed.pdf (accessed 26 October 2009).

[15] Age Discrimination, *The Free Dictionary*. Online: http://legal-dictionary.thefreedictionary.com/Age+Discrimination (accessed 26 October 2009).

[16] One suspects many will not retire as the distinction between work and leisure blurs in the academic profession. In the eloquently argued *The Last Professor*, Frank Donoghue expresses a widely held sentiment that he "intend[s] never to retire..." (New York: Fordham University Press, 2009),

xix. The *coup de grâce* is that many near-retirement professors from the baby boom generation have discovered that their pension funds have drastically shrunken in the wake of the financial collapse that began in September 2008. As reported by David W. Breneman, professor of the economics of education at the University of Virginia, "One might also speculate, if a severe recession does ensue, that... faculty members nearing retirement may decide to keep teaching for more years than they had planned, increasing the financial burden on their institutions." "Commentary: What Colleges Can Learn from Recessions Past," *The Chronicle of Higher Education*, 10 October 2008, A112; Sierra Millman, "AAUP Study Examines Faculty Retirement," *The Chronicle of Higher Education*, 23 March 2007, A10.

With price rigidities of the Keynesian sort (another distortion), academic salaries are not adjusted downward. Inasmuch as senior tenured professors tend to be at the top of the pay scale, what gives in university budgets are job openings. The Academic Year 2008–2009 was the worst labor market in almost every academic field. Newly minted doctorates, post-doctorates, and post-post doctorates were effectively locked out of tenure-track academic careers. Is it efficient? Is it equitable? The theory of second best would reply in the negative.

[17] Paul A. Samuelson and William D. Nordhaus, *ECONOMICS*, 18th ed. (New York: McGraw-Hill, 2005), 188.

[18] Nicholas Dawidoff, "The Civil Heretic," *The New York Times Magazine*, 29 March 2009, 32. Online: http://www.nytimes.com/2009/03/29/magazine/29Dyson-t.html?_r=1&scp=1&sq=dyson%20climate%20change%20magazine&st=cse (accessed 2 November 2009).

[19] Garrett Hardin, "The Tragedy of the Commons," *Science* 162 (1968): 1243–1248.

[20] Aida Arteaga. "El insólito del Mecanismo de Desarrollo Limpio," Masters of Environmental Studies thesis, FLACSO-Ecuador, May 2002.

[21] Robert William Fogel and Stanley L. Engerman *Time on the Cross: Evidence and Methods – A Supplement* (Boston: Little, Brown and Co., 1974), 8.

[22] Fogel and Engerman, *Time on the Cross: The Economics*, 11.

[23] Ironically, one of the most cogent criticisms against *Time on the Cross* is that Fogel and Engerman committed the error of small sample size, relying on the statistics compiled from just one plantation. Herbert G. Gutman, *Slavery and the Numbers Game: A Critique of 'Time on the Cross'* (Champaign, Ill.: University of Illinois Press, 2003).

[24] Peter Monaghan, "Taking on 'Rational Man': Dissident Economists Fight for a Niche in the Discipline," *The Chronicle of Higher Education*, 24 January 2003.

[25] At the Inaugural Audience of The International Tribunal of Climate Justice convened in Cochabamba, Bolivia 13–14 October 2009, six of the eight jurors did not know the economic meaning of "market failure," one of whom was otherwise well grounded in the scientific literature of climate change. Although aware of *The Stern Review*, market failure did not penetrate the consciousness of that juror. I was unable to convince my fellow jurors to incorporate any reference that "'market failure' is cost-shifting success" in the final ruling. Similarly, I could not persuade them to distinguish between a carbon market that finances "false solutions" (their term for leakages or

second best) and one that enables gains from trade, such is the obtuseness of economics or my ineffectiveness as a teacher.

[26] Nicholas Stern, *The Economics of Climate Change: The Stern Review* (New York: Cambridge, 2006), 52 and 185, respectively.

[27] E. O. Wilson, "Introduction: Life is a Narrative" in *The Best American Science and Nature Writing 2001*, E. O. Wilson and Burkhard Bilger, eds. (New York: Houghton Mifflin Company, 2001), xii–xx, xviii.

[28] Richard Dawkins so identifies the fallacy in the "proofs" of the existence of God. *The God Delusion* (New York: A Mariner Book: Houghton Mifflin Company, 2006), 109.

[29] Benjamin S. Bloom, *Taxonomy of Educational Objectives, Handbook I: The Cognitive Domain* (New York: David McKay Co Inc., 1956).

[30] It is a conclusion that most good teachers eventually stumble upon. The Nobel Laureate in Physics Richard P. Feynman remarked that when on a Fulbright scholarship in Brazil he "finally figured out that the students had memorized everything, but they didn't know what anything meant. When they heard 'light that is reflected from a medium with an index,' they didn't know that it meant a matter *such as water*" [italics in original], *Surely You're Joking, Mr. Feynman!* (New York: W.W. Norton, 1985), 212.

[31] Jerome Barkow, Leda Cosmides and John Tooby, *The Adapted Mind* (New York: Oxford University Press, 1992).

[32] Garrett Hardin, *Living Within Limits* (New York: Oxford University Press, 1993), 15.

[33] Dawidoff, op. cit.

[34] Jacques Ellul, *Propaganda: The Formation of Men's Attitudes*, Konrad Kellen and Jean Lerner, trans. (New York: Vintage Books, 1965), 124–26.

Chapter 5

[1] In economics, one can go back to Adam Smith and compare his day with that of Hobbes. Stephen A. Marglin, *The Dismal Science: How Thinking Like an Economist Undermines Community* (Cambridge, Massachusetts: Harvard University Press, 2008), 64.

[2] Stephen A. Marglin, "Why Economists are Part of the Problem," *The Chronicle of Higher Education*, 27 February 2009. The usual statistic for the US is one quarter but, as Marglin argues, one must consider that 25% of the labor force was in the agricultural sector where prices bottomed out, effectively putting them into a poverty equivalent to joblessness.

[3] John Maynard Keynes, *The General Theory of Employment, Interest and Money* (London: MacMillan. 1936).

[4] Nicholas Stern, *The Economics of Climate Change: The Stern Review* (New York: Cambridge, 2006), xv.

[5] Ibid, 27.

[6] I use the metaphor in the sense that E. O. Wilson uses it in his chapter "The Bottleneck," *The Future of Life* (New York: Vintage Books, 2002), 22.

[7] Stern, op. cit., 512.

[8] As I prepare the final manuscript, the Committee for the Nobel Memorial Prize in Economics announces Elinor Ostrom as the 2009 Laureate "for her analysis of economic governance, especially the commons." Criticism of Hardin's "Tragedy of the Commons" has been the trampoline for much of her analysis. Hardin never won the Nobel. Online: http://nobelprize.org/nobel_prizes/economics/laureates/2009/ (accessed 26 October 2009).

[9] Garrett Hardin, "Lifeboat Ethics: the Case Against Helping the Poor," *Psychology Today*, September 1974. Online: http://www.garrett hardinsociety.org/articles/art_lifeboat_ethics_case_against_helping_poor. html (accessed on 26 October 2009).

[10] Marglin, *The Dismal Science*, 50.

[11] Hardin, op. cit.

[12] Ibid.

[13] Government of Bolivia, "Paper No. 8 Commitments for Annex I Parties under paragraph 1(b)(i) of the Bali Action Plan: Evaluating developed countries' historical climate debt to developing countries," April 2009, 46–47.

[14] Hardin, op. cit.

[15] "Since 1750 the emission of greenhouse gases has increased significantly as the result of human activities." Government of Bolivia, op. cit., 46.

[16] The issue of damages to the economically poor carbon-poor countries requires an international tribunal of climate justice.

[17] The similar endeavor is UN-REDD (United Nations Collaborative Programme on Reducing Emissions from Deforestation and Forest Degradation in Developing Countries). FAO, UNDP, UNEP Framework Document June 2008. *Reduction of Emissions through Deforestation and Degradation).* Online: http://www.undp.org/mdtf/UN-REDD/overview. shtml (accessed 27 October 2009).

[18] Ad Hoc Working Group on Long-Term Cooperative Action under the Convention Fulfillment of The Bali Action Plan and Components of the Agreed Outcome, Paper No. 16. Quito, Ecuador, April 2009.

[19] It is an analog with NIMTO (not-in-my-term-of-office) which is a derivate of NIMBY (not-in-my-back-yard). Joseph Henry Vogel, "Reflecting Financial and Other Incentives of the TMOIFGR: The Biodiversity Cartel" in *A Moving Target: Genetic Resources and Options for Tracking and Monitoring their International Flows,* Manuel Ruiz and Isabel Lapeña, eds. (Gland, Switzerland: IUCN, 2007), 47–74. Online: http://data.iucn.org/dbtw-wpd/edocs/EPLP-067-3.pdf (accessed 26 October 2009).

[20] Matt Finer, Remi Monce, and Clinton Jenkins, "Leaving the Oil Under the Amazon: Ecuador's Yasuní-ITT Initiative," *Biotropica*, 26 October 2009. Online: http://www3.interscience.wiley.com/journal/122664071/abstract? CRETRY=1&SRETRY=0 (accessed Oct. 28, 2009).

[21] Editorial, "Preventable Deaths," *The New York Times*, 30 May 2009, A18 or Rizvi, Haider, "Finance: Aid Loss Prompting Development Emergency," *Inter Press Service News Agency*, 17 Sept. 2009. Online: http://www. ipsnews.net/news.asp?idnews =48477 (accessed 26 October 2009).

[22] Peter May, email message to author, 28 May 2009.

[23] Discounting is a deathblow to species in threatened habitats. David Ehrenfeld, "Why Put a Value on Biodiversity?" in *Biodiversity*, E. O. Wilson and Frances M. Peter, eds. (Washington, D.C.: National Academy Press, 1988), 213.

[24] This conclusion is quickly reached with any good command of ECON101. Sven Wunder, "How Do We Deal With Leakage?" in *Moving Ahead with REDD: Issues, Options, and Implications*, Arild Angelsen, ed (Bogor, Indonesia: CIFOR, 2008), 65–76.

[25] John Maynard Keynes, *A Tract on Monetary Reform*, (London: MacMillan, 1924), 80.

[26] Keynes, *The General Theory*, viii.

[27] Upton Sinclair, quoted in Al Gore, *An Inconvenient Truth: The Planetary Emergency of Global Warming and What We Can Do About* (New York: Rodale, 2006), 266–267.

[28] Alan S. Blinder, "Is Government too Political?" *Foreign Affairs*, November/ December 1997, 115–126.

[29] Global Health and Global Development Programs and Partnerships of The Bill and Melinda Gates Foundation. Online: http://www.gatesfoundation. org/global-development/Pages/overview.aspx (accessed 26 October 2009).

[30] Marglin, "Why Economists are Part of the Problem."

[31] Unless in the context of a denunciation, "lebensraum" is taboo even though its second meaning may be intended: "space required for life, growth, or activity." Online: http://www.merriam-webster.com/dictionary/leben sraum (accessed 26 October 2009).

[32] This is not the same as the misnamed "Payment of Environmental Services" (PES). Most PES programs lack title in the legal sense – people are being paid for things they do not own! However, one can pay for protection of environmental services. See Joseph Henry Vogel, "¿Mercados o Metáforas? Pagos por Servicios Ambientales en Pimampiro, Eucador. Estudio de un caso en el Ecuador" in *Valoración económica, ecológica y ambiental. Análisis de casos en Iberoamérica*, Rosi Ulate y Jesús Cisneros, eds. (Editorial Universidad Heredia, Costa Rica: Nacional EUNA, 2007), 521–566. Examples of payment for protecting environmental services exist in Ecuador, see Restoring Natural Capital RNC Alliance. Online: http://www.rncalliance.org/epages/ rncalliance.sf/?ObjectPath=/Shops/rncalliance (accessed 26 October 2009).

[33] Stern, op. cit., 238.

[34] Although as early as the mid-1970s the government of Costa Rica committed to preserving 25% of its natural habitat, the system did not become fully protected *de facto* until the creation of the Sistema Nacional de Areas de Conservación (SINAC) in 1998, meaning that the relevant HDI category for REDD is the same as for the Yasuní Initiative, viz., High Human Development Category. Online: http://www.costarica-nationalparks.com/ (accessed 26 October 2009).

[35] World Rainforest Movement, "Ecuador: Zero community benefits from FACE PROFAFOR certified plantations." Online: http://www.wrm.org.uy/ bulletin/108/Ecuador_FACE_PROFAFOR.html (accessed 27 October 2009).

[36] For a thorough analysis of *ciclovías* and sustainable development in the Ecuadorian context, see Catalina Noroña, "De la Bicicleta a la utopía: la

construcción de organizaciones socio-ambientales desde las propuestas de transporte alternative - el caso de Quito, Ecuador," Masters Thesis, FLACSO-Ecuador, Quito, 2009.

[37] Paulo Freire, *Pedagogy of the Oppressed* (New York: Continuum Publishing Company, 1970).

[38] Andrew C. Revkin, "A New Measure of Well-Being from a Happy Little Kingdom," *The New York Times*, 4 October 2005.

[39] "A former postal worker commits mass murder," *History Made Every Day*, 10 October 1991. Online: http://www.history.com/this-day-in-history.do?action=tdihArticleCategory&display Date=10/10&categoryId=crime(accessed 27 October 2009).

[40] Stern, op. cit., 247.

[41] S. Pacala and R. Socolow "Stabilization Wedges: Solving the Climate Problem for the Next Fifty Years with Current Technologies." *Science* 305(2004): 968–72.

[42] Paul R. Ehrlich and Anne H. Ehrlich, *The Dominant Animal* (Washington, D.C.: Island Press, 2009), 281.

[43] Garrett Hardin, *Living Within Limits* (New York: Oxford University Press, 1993), 3.

[44] Sven Wunder, *Oil Wealth and the Fate of the Forest* (London: Routgledge, 2003), 368.

[45] Joseph Henry Vogel, 'The Tragedy of the Commons': A Museum of Bioprospecting, Intellectual Property Rights, and the Public Domain," in *The Nexus of Law and Biology: New Ethical Challenges*, Barbara A. Hocking, ed (London: Ashgate, 2009), 75–84.

[46] Joseph Henry Vogel, ed, *The Biodiversity Cartel: Transforming Traditional Knowledge into Trade Secrets* (Quito, Ecuador: The InterAmerican Development Bank/Consejo Nacional de Desarrollo, CARE, USAID, SANREM, and EcoCiencia, 2000).

[47] Joseph Henry Vogel, Janny Robles, Camilo Gomides, and Carlos Muñiz, "Geopiracy as an Emerging Issue in Intellectual Property Rights: The Rationale for Leadership by Small States," *Tulane Environmental Law Journal* 21 (Spring 2008): 391–406.

[48] More formally known as "The Fundamental Paradox of Egoistic Hedonism," Henry Sidgwick, *The Methods of Ethics* (Indianapolis: Hackett Publishing Co, 1981 [first published 1907]). Pleasure is attained not through its own pursuit, but as a byproduct of work. See, "Hedonism" in *Stanford Encyclopedia* of *Philosophy*. Online: http://plato.stanford.edu/entries/hedonism/ (accessed 27 October 2009).

[49] *SIERRA* Magazine, 94:1, January/February 2009, 86.

[50] Connie Rogers, "Feathers, Fur and Jungle Waters," *The New York Times Travel Section*, 1 August 2004, Section 5, 1, 8, 13.

[51] Ibid, 13.

[52] Redacción Sociedad, "Tursimo: La crisis en EE.UU. es una gran oportunidad,"*El Comercio*, 4 January 2009, 1–2.

[53] The choices themselves can be best understood from the paradigm of evolutionary psychology. Gad Saad, *The Evolutionary Bases of Consumption* (Mahwah, New Jersey: Lawrence Erlbaum Associates, Publihsers, 2007).

[54] "Coca-Cola+Mentos en el Colegio Aleman." Online: http://www.
youtube.com/watch?v=8TR6xvtj5SY (accessed 27 October 2009).

[55] "Expalsa, Our Social Responsibility." Online: http://www.youtube.com/
watch?v=6T134zSZjGM&feature=related (accessed 27 October 2009).

[56] Whether or not there is a basis for the video can be easily vetted by panels of
experts. The "fair trade" movement can be seen in Ecuador for coffee and
banana production. Online: http://www.youtube.com/watch?v=20 Prlca
T1a0 and http://www.youtube.com/watch?v=mrp7FpJGyqw (accessed 27
October 2009).

[57] Loggers in Canada do not touch the forests that border the highways,
thereby fooling passing cars of the devastation just beyond view. Andre
Carothers, "Brazil of the North: How the British Columbia Timber Company
Macmillan-Bloedel Escapes Responsibility for Destroying Ancient Forests,"
E Magazine, 1 April 1994. Online: http://www.encyclopedia.com/doc/1G1-
14896050.html (accessed 27 October 2009).

[58] Marisa López-Rivera, "Faculty Raises Are Down Slightly from Last Year,"
The Chronicle of Higher Education, 13 March 2009. Statistics computed from
table "Average Faculty Salaries by Field and Rank at 4 Year Colleges and
Universities, 2008–9." The Fulbright Program attempts to thwart criticism by
disclosing in the last of website FAQs "Fulbright grants are not intended to
approach salaries." Online: http://www.cies.org/us_scholars/us_awards/
FAQs.htm#12 (accessed on 27 October 2009).

Conclusions

[1] The commonplace is also a book title. Obama for America, *Change we Can
Believe In: Barack Obama's Plan to Renew America's Promise* (New York: Three
Rivers Press, 2008).

[2] "I've already said I'm happy to see us move forward on increasing
domestic production, including offshore drilling – but we can't do that in
isolation from all these other important steps that need to be taken."
"Interview with President Obama on Climate Bill," *The New York Times*,
28 June 2009.

[3] A point made by Deidre McCloskey and taken to heart. "Most academic
prose, from both students and faculty, could use more humor." *Economical
Writing*, 2nd ed. (Long Grove, Illinois: Waveland Press, 2002), 43.

[4] Nicholas Georgescu-Roegen, "Energy and Economic Myths," *Southern
Economic Journal* 41 no. 3 (January 1975). Online: http://dieoff.org/
page148.htm (accessed 27 October 2009).

[5] E. O. Wilson, *The Future of Life* (New York: Vintage Books, 2002), 7.

[6] Charles Darwin, *The Origin of Species*, intro. by J. W. Burrow (Baltimore:
Penguin, 1968 1859]), 462.

[7] "Many Scientists Believe Runaway Greenhouse Effect Possible." Online:
http://archive.greenpeace.org/climate/database/records/zgpz0638.html
(accessed 27 October 2009).

[8] Carl Sagan, Ann Druyan, and Steven Soter. *Cosmos Episode 13 "Who Speaks For Earth?"* Public Broadcasting Service, 55 min, 20 sec. Online: http://www.videosift.com/video/Carl-Sagan-Cosmos-13-Who-Speaks-for-Earth (accessed 27 October 2009).

[9] Ibid.

[10] European Space Agency, "Climate and Evolution," 28 November 2007. Online:http://www.esa.int/SPECIALS/Venus_Express/SEMGK373R8F_0.html (accessed 27 October 2009).

[11] David Chandler, "Climate Change Odds Much Worse than Previously Thought: New Analysis Shows Warming Could be Double Previous Estimates," *MIT News*, 19 May 2009. Online:http://web.mit.edu/newsoffice/2009/roulette-0519.html (accessed 27 October 2009).

[12] Carl Sagan, *The Cosmic Connection: An Extraterrestrial Perspective* (New York: Dell Publishing, 1973), 237–38.

[13] Earthrise from Apollo 8 (1968) or The Blue Marble from Apollo 17 (1972). Online:http://www.abc.net.au/science/moon/earthrise.htm and http://svs.gsfc.nasa.gov/vis/a000000/a002600/a002680/ (accessed 28 October 2009).

[14] One imagines effete make-up artists scurrying about the stage with a briefcase of ties from which to choose.

[15] With reference to the first of the trilogy: "…'stability' another useful term of political discourse, which translates as 'Whatever serves the interests of power.'" With reference to the last: "It is perhaps worth mentioning that the word 'profits' has largely disappeared from respectable discourse. In contemporary Newspeak, the word is to be pronounced 'jobs.'"Noam Chomsky, *Powers and Prospects: Reflection on Human Nature and the Social Order* (London: Pluto Press, 1996), 133 and 103.

[16] Transcript: Obama's G-20 Press Conference, 2 April 2009. Online: http://www.cbsnews.com/stories/2009/04/02/politics/100days/worldaffairs/main4914735.shtml (accessed 27 October 2009).

[17] "Thunderous" was the adjective Donald Mann used to describe the oxymoron of "sustainable economic growth" for which Obama's "sustainable growth" is merely a short-hand. "Reflection on Sustainable Development," *Human Survival*, 15 (1989), 2.

[18] Jacques Ellul, *Propaganda: The Formation of Men's Attitudes*, trans. Konrad Kellen and Jean Lerner (New York: Vintage Books, 1965), 138.

[19] For an online background on The Club of Rome: http://www.cluboofrome.org/eng/about/3/ (accessed 27 October 2009).

[20] Donella H. Meadows, Dennis L. Meadows, Jørgen Randers and William W. Behrens III, *The Limits to Growth* (New York: Universe Books, 1972).

[21] Paul Krugman, "Betraying the Planet," *The New York Times*, 28 June 2009, A21.

[22] John Broder, "Obama Opposes Trade Sanctions in Climate Bill" *The New York Times*, 29 June 2009, A1.

[23] John Broder, "House Passes Bill to Address Threat of Climate Change," *The New York Times*, 27 June 2009, A1.

[24] Ibid.

[25] Ibid.

[26] Ibid.

Appendix

[1] Henry Jenkins, "From YouTube to YouNiversity," *The Chronicle Review* 53, 16 February 2007, 9.

[2] Garrett Hardin, "The Tragedy of the Commons," *Science* 162 (1968): 1243–1248.

[3] Joseph Henry Vogel, "Ecocriticism as an Economic School of Thought: Woody Allen's Match Point as Exemplary." *OMETECA Science and Humanities* XII (2008): 105–119.

[4] Camilo Gomides, "Putting a New Definition of Ecocriticism to the Test: *The Case of the Burning Season*, a Film (Mal)Adaptation." *Interdisciplinary Studies in Literature and Environment* 13 no. 1 (2006): 13–23, 16.

[5] The Open Vision Community (an Educational Resource for the New Age), http://openvision.org/content/story-stuff (accessed 27 October 2009).

INDEX